BANGLA RANNA

THE BENGAL COOKBOOK

(Second Revised Edition)

BANGLA RANNA
THE BENGAL COOKBOOK

(Second Revised Edition)

Minakshie DasGupta

UBSPD
UBS Publishers' Distributors Pvt. Ltd.
New Delhi • Bangalore • Kolkata • Chennai • Patna • Bhopal
Ernakulam • Mumbai • Lucknow • Pune • Hyderabad

UBS Publishers' Distributors Pvt. Ltd.

5 Ansari Road, New Delhi-110 002
Phones: 011-23273601, 23266646 • Fax: 23276593, 23274261
E-mail: ubspd@ubspd.com

10 First Main Road, Gandhi Nagar, Bangalore-560 009
Phones: 080-22253903, 22263901, 22263902 • Fax: 22263904
E-mail: ubspdbng@eth.net

8/1-B Chowringhee Lane, Kolkata-700 016
Phones: 033-22521821, 22522910, 22529473 • Fax: 22523027
E-mail: ubspdcal@cal.vsnl.net.in

60 Nelson Manickam Road, Aminjikarai, Chennai-600 029
Phones: 044-23746222, 23746351-2 • Fax: 23746287
E-mail: ubspd@che.ubspd.com

Ground Floor, Western Side, Annaporna Complex, 202 Naya Tola,
Patna-800 004 • Phones: 0612-2672856, 2673973, 2686170
Fax: 2686169 • E-mail: ubspdpat1@sancharnet.in

143, M.P. Nagar, Zone-I, Bhopal-462 011
Phones: 0755-5203183, 5203193, 2555228 • Fax: 2555285
E-mail: ubspdbhp@sancharnet.in

No. 40/7940, Convent Road, Ernakulam-682 035
Phones: 0484-2353901, 2363905 • Fax: 2365511
E-mail: ubspdekm@asianetindia.com

2nd Floor, Apeejay Chambers, 5 Wallace Street, Fort,
Mumbai-400 001 • Phones: 022-56376922, 56376923
Fax: 56376921• E-mail: ubspdmum@mum.ubspd.com

1st Floor, Halwasiya Court Annexe, 11-MG Marg, Hazaratganj,
Lucknow-226 001 • Phones: 0522-2294134, 2611128
Fax: 2294133 • E-mail: ubspdlko@lko.ubspd.com

680 Budhwar Peth, 2nd floor, Appa Balwant Chowk, Pune-411 002
Phone: 020-4028920 • Fax: 020-4028921
E-mail: ubspdpune@rediffmail.com

NVK Towers, 2nd floor, 3-6-272, Himayat Nagar,
Hyderabad-500029 • Phones: 040-23262572, 23262573, 23262574
Fax: 040-23262572 • E-mail: ubspdhyd@vsnl.net

Visit us at www.ubspd.com & www.gobookshopping.com

© Minakshie DasGupta

First Published	1982	Fifth Reprint	2001
Second Revised Edition	1998	Sixth Reprint	2002
First Reprint	1999	Seventh Reprint	2002
Second Reprint	1999	Eighth Reprint	2003
Third Reprint	2000	Ninth Reprint	2004
Fourth Reprint	2001	Tenth Reprint	2004
		Eleventh Reprint	2005

Photographs: Dilip Sinha
Food Stylist: Rakhi P. Dasgupta

Printed at: Nutech Photolithographers, Delhi

In memory of my mother,
Shantilata Ghose,
who taught me to appreciate
my heritage

I dedicate this book to
my husband, Mitu
and my children, Pia Promina,
Chandradip and Rakhi Purnima,
my severest critics and
greatest admirers

Contents

Introduction to the Second Edition   ix

Introduction to the First Edition   1

Eating the Bengali Way
Order of eating — a ritual   3

General Instructions
Including preparation of *chhana*, coconut milk, *dahi*
and special Bengali *masalas* like *panch phoran*
and *garam masala*   5

Glossary
In English, Bengali and Hindi   9

Aunno — Cereals
Rice, *Khichuri, Ghee Bhat, Luchi* etc.   13

Dal
Lentils, pulses and legumes   23

Tarkari — Vegetables
The art of vegetarian cooking   35

Maach — Fish
The Bengali's favourite food   97

Mangsho, Murgi O Dim — Meat, Chicken and Eggs
An addition to the Bengali cuisine   141

Anglo-Indian Recipes
Western influence on Bengali cuisine   161

Ambol, Tauk, Achar — Chutneys and Pickles
To tickle the palate   175

Jal Khabar — Snacks
A ritual of a more leisurely past   189

Mishti — Sweets
Renowned throughout India   197

Paan O Moshla
Betel leaf with selected spices — a digestive   213

Index
Arranged alphabetically under section headings   215

Introduction to the Second Edition

Our Mother, Minakshie DasGupta, wrote this book in the memory of her mother, Shantilata Ghose. It gives us great pleasure to release the second edition of this book in her Birth Centenary year.

We dedicate this edition of Bangla Ranna to all the super cooks in our family: Thakurma (grandaunt), Dimma (grandmother), Maa (the author of this book), our brother Chandradip, Pabitrada, and Giridhari, our cook. They have left us an invaluable heritage and the enormous task of perpetuating their memory through gourmet cuisine.

PIA PROMINA DASGUPTA BARVE
RAKHI PURNIMA DASGUPTA

Introduction to the First Edition

Many of us have enjoyed food from other parts of India. Many of us would like to try those recipes in our own homes. My desire to know about the foods of others and the eagerness of my friends to learn more about the food of Bengal have prompted me to write this book.

I was fortunate to have been born into a family of gourmets and even more fortunate to have married into another. As the families had ties with both East and West Bengal, I had the opportunity of appreciating the richness of both cuisines.

The cooking in Bengal varies greatly between the East and the West. The adventurous East Bengali housewife has more to offer in variety and taste, whereas the West Bengali excels in the preparation of sweets for which Bengal is renowned.

The Bengali housewife is frugal and abhors waste of any kind. By making use of every part of a fish or vegetable, she plays her part in contributing to an economical budget. For instance, the bones and head of a fish will be used to transform a *dal* or vegetable dish, while even the peel of certain vegetables make a delectable dish in its own right. Great stress is laid on the *correct* way of cutting and preparing vegetables and this is as much a part of the Art of Bengali Cooking as the actual cooking itself. Spices are used very delicately to give each dish its own subtle flavour, but can always be varied according to taste.

To the Bengalis who may read this book, I would mention that although the way I have shown of cooking a particular dish may differ from theirs, it is nonetheless authentic and in many cases the recipe has been in my family for generations. Nor do I say that mine is the only authentic form. A recipe for the same dish varies, from family to family, the world over.

I lay no claim on the originality of the recipes presented in this book. It would not be traditional Bengali fare had I done so. I have, however, tried to present the recipes in a more scientific way than the traditional method of "*a little bit of this and a pinch of that...*" in which many of us were taught. Wherever possible, I have tried to incorporate the use of modern cooking aids such as pressure cookers, household foil and liquidisers; and by suggesting substitutes for ingredients, I hope to bring this book within the orbit of many who may have been deterred by the unavailability of original ingredients. The adventurous and innovative cook will, I am sure, find other and perhaps better substitutes for herself than those mentioned.

I take this opportunity to thank all those friends and relatives who have provided me with family recipes. I have tried to give credit for this wherever possible. In particular, I must thank my friends—Kiki, Premila Lal who encouraged me to write this book; and for more practical assistance in editing the manuscript, Jaya Chaliha who made it possible for me to complete the book. The original manuscript, which has lain in cold storage for eleven years, has now been condensed to presentable proportions and my grateful thanks go to Mihir K. Das who has supervised the production of this book; and to my daughter Pia, who took on the marathon task of re-editing the manuscript in a very short time.

Finally, I would like to thank the Typist, who wishes to remain anonymous, for his patience in typing and re-typing the manuscript in record time. I would also like to thank all my friends, too numerous to mention individually, for the time and effort they have given in my being able to complete and give the book for printing.

Calcutta   MINAKSHIE DASGUPTA
1st Baisak, 1389
15th April, 1982

Eating the Bengali Way

A meal, for the Bengali, is a ritual in itself even if it is only boiled rice and lentils *(dal bhat)*, with of course a little fish. Bengalis, like the French, spend not only a great deal of time thinking about food but also on its preparation and eating. Quips like "Bengalis live to eat" and "Bengalis spend most of their income on food" are exaggerated, but some of the stories of the Bengali clerk reporting late at the office because his spiced fish stew *(maacher jhol)* was not ready on time, is a truism of the past.

The early morning shopping for fresh vegetables, fish etc. is the prerogative of the head of the family, because he feels that he alone can pick up the best at a bargain price. Even in affluent households, the head of the family is often seen in the market place on Sunday mornings, busily making the choicest purchases for his Sunday lunch, after which he will enjoy his siesta.

Stress is laid on how the food is served and the order followed. Each item is expected to be eaten separately with a little rice so that the flavours are not mixed. Generally, rice is served first along with a little salt, a piece of lime and green chillies placed on the right hand side. The first item may be a little *ghee* which is poured over a small portion of the rice and eaten with a pinch of salt. The bitter preparation, *shukto*, is then served, although this is normally done only in the afternoon. After this comes lentils or *dal*, together with roasted or fried vegetables *(bhaja, bhate or bharta)*. Next come the vegetable dishes, the lightly spiced vegetables, *chenchki, chokka, misti dalna*, followed by the more heavily spiced *dalna, ghonto* and those cooked with fish. Then come the fish preparations. Again the lightly spiced dishes first, for instance *macher jhol*, followed by various other preparations and climaxed with prawn or crayfish dishes. Finally chicken or mutton, if this is being served at all. *Chutney (ambal or tauk)* with its sweet-sour flavour comes next to clear the palate together with crisp savoury wafers, *papadum* or *papar*. Dessert is usually sweet yogurt *(misti doi)*. But on special occasions, *doi* may be replaced by *payesh*, a rice pudding with a difference! The meal is finally concluded with the handing out of betel leaf *(paan)* which is considered to be an aid to digestion and an astringent.

Traditionally, a meal is served on a large gun-metal or silver plate *(thala)* and the various items of food are placed in bowls *(batis)* around the top of the *thala*, running from left to right. Rice is mounded in a neat round and placed on the middle of the *thala*, with a little salt, chillies and lime placed on the upper right hand corner. A glass of water is always placed on the right hand side. It is normal to sit on the floor and eat. Cutlery is not used as we eat with the fingers of the right hand and strict etiquette is observed with regard to this. Today, of course, in most homes people eat on a dining table and ceramic or earthen plates are used instead of the traditional gun-metal. *Batis* are not placed for everyday meals. Normally the lady of the house or servant serves the food. Today's hostess will more often serve a buffet dinner or lunch. But special occasions still see the revival of the ritual.

I should perhaps mention that certain preparations are usually served at the mid-day meal. The bitter preparations, *bhates, poras* or *bhartas*, the lighter spiced vegetable dishes and the smaller variety of whole fish, are preferably eaten at lunch. For the evening meal, deep-fried puffed bread *(luchis)* are a popular cereal. On special occasions, a light pilaff *(Ghee Bhat)* is served with curried carp *(rui)* or meat or chicken curry.

For the reader's convenience, I suggest here some typical menus for lunch and dinner both for everyday meals and also for special occasions.

Everyday lunch menus

Rice	Rice
Tauk dal	Masur dal
Begun bhaja	Alu bhaja
Palang sager ghanto	Bandhakopir misti dalna
Doi maach	Rui maacher jhol
Aam jhol	Peper chutney
Misti doi	Misti doi

Everyday dinner menus

Luchi or rice	Alu chops with salad
Potol bhaja	Rice
Cholar dal	Mug dal/a light vegetable
Alu-phulkopir dalna	curry preparation
Mangshor curry	Jhal-firazee
Misti	Malpoa

Lunch 'Special'

Rice	Rice
Mug dal	Shukto
Elish maach tetul	Matar dal
bhaja	Begun bharta
Mochar ghanto	Enchorer dalna
Monama	Daab chingri
Pixie's special fish	Tomato chutney
curry	Dio/
Tomato chutney	Rossogolla
Payesh	

Dinner for special occasions

Luchi/Ghee bhat	Smoked hilsa
Misti mug dal	Paratha
Begun bhaja	Cholar dal
Bandhakopir dalna	Kabab
Potoler dolma with	Green salad
shrimps	Spring onions, green
Rui maacher kalia	chillies and lime
Mangshor gota mashla	Alu dom
Alubokhara chutney	Bhapa doi
Rossogollar payesh	

General Instructions

In order to simplify and make *Bangla Ranna* practical to my readers, I give below the ground work on which these recipes are based.

Weights and Measures

A weighing scale is usually absent in a Bengali housewife's kitchen. However, I would advise an adventurous cook to invest in one as it helps towards better results when the ingredients are exactly measured.

As all housewives do not possess scales, I have given measures in cups and spoons.

The following are the conversions:

Solid Measure—using level cupfuls in standard cup measures:

Ingredients	Grams	Cups
Rice	500	2½ approx.
Flour	500	4 approx.
Sugar	500	2 approx.
Dal	500	2½ approx.
Ghee/oil	500	2¼ approx.

Liquid Measures given in standard measuring cups:
1 standard measuring cup = 2 teacups

Spoon measures

Given below are equivalents for standard spoon measures using the modern stainless steel tableware commonly used in India:

1 tablespoon = 1 dessert spoon (or spoon used for eating)
1 teaspoon   = 1 teaspoon
⅛ teaspoon = a pinch

Bangla Ranna Microwave

The microwave cooker has heralded one of the most important cooking revolutions of our times. The unbelievable speed with which it can defrost, cook fresh food, or reheat prepared dishes brings an immediacy to cooking that complies with today's time-conscious lifestyle.

The recipes mentioned in this book have been tested and cooked on a 600 watts (output) microwave cooker. If the microwave you are using has a different wattage, please check with your instruction booklet as to how much time, more or less, is needed for any given dish. Please remember the times quoted are approximate; the initial temperature and the size of container will always effect cooking time. Therefore always check foods before the end of the time quoted. Time can always be added, but never taken away. Oven-ware glass, china, all-over glazed earthenware and stoneware are all suitable for microwave cooking. Today special microwave cookware is also available including browning dishes etc.

However most of the microwave recipes in Bangla Ranna do not need to be browned.

If using cling film to cover the cooking containers, pierce the cling film to prevent ballooning during heat expansion, to allow steam to escape.

Fuel

Traditionally coal or wood was generally used for cooking. Today bottle gas and kerosene stoves which can be regulated are growing in popularity and are used extensively in cities and towns. The recipes in this book have been prepared on electric and gas cookers. The temperatures, where indicated, are given in Fahrenheit.

Utensils

You do not require any special utensils for Bengali cooking. The *dekchi* referred to in these recipes is merely a saucepan without a handle and can be substituted by the same or by a pan. The *karai* is found in all Indian kitchens. It was formerly made of iron but is being rapidly replaced by aluminium or stainless steel. Today copper bottom 'non-stick' *karais* are available too. The *karai* is deep and hemispherical in shape with two handles and is similar to a Chinese *wok*. It can be easily replaced by any other suitable utensil in your kitchen. The *tawa* (or griddle) is a heavy circular iron plate which is used for making *porotas* etc. A heavy frying pan or an electric plate can be substituted. The *thala* (or *thali*) is a large circular plate which is used in the kitchen and for eating. It is usually made of metal but marble and stone *thalas* are also used.

Stirrers

Stirring is usually done with a *check hatha* or flattened metal spoon except where a wooden spoon is indicated. A *jhanjri* or flat slotted spoon is used for frying luchis etc.

Sautéing is usually done with a *khunti*, a long handled implement with a flat thin bell-shaped piece.

Kitchen Aids

The *Sheelnora*—grinding stone, a slab of 16 inches × 10 inches and a small bolster-shaped stone roller 9 inches long. Both the slab and roller are chipped from time to time as with use they are worn smooth. *A hamal dista*—mortar and pestle, can be used instead of the *sheelnora*.

These aids are primarily used for grinding spices to a fine powder or fine paste with the addition of water. Today liquidisers/grinders have replaced these age-old aids in many homes. To use a liquidiser successfully for grinding spices to the desired consistency, dry grind all the spices and then liquidise with a small quantity of water to get a fine paste. Before grinding, it is better to oven or pan roast the spices dry. Turmeric should be broken into little pieces before grinding.

Spices

Herein lies the heart and soul of Bengali cooking. Spices must NOT be used with a heavy hand. The Bengali believes that it is the way in which you grind the spices that either makes or mars his food. Hence great stress is laid on how the spices are ground, on the amount of water used and on the *fineness* to which the spices are ground. Unless otherwise stated, water is used to grind the spices to a paste.

2 average pieces turmeric ground with 3 tablespoons water = 2 tablespoons (approx.) ground paste

1 tablespoon cummin seed or coriander seed ground with 2½ tablespoons water = 2 tablespoons (approx.) ground paste

1 tablespoon mustard seed ground with 2 tablespoons water = 2 tablespoons (approx.) ground paste

Dry Ground Spices

Though freshly ground spices are prepared in Bangla Ranna, dry ground spices may be used quite successfully.

Method

Use ⅓ the amount of wet ground spices indicated in the recipe. Mix to a paste using sufficient water.

Dry Mustard Powder

Colmans mustard powder, mixed to a paste, may be substituted for freshly ground mustard—use only *half* the quantity mentioned in the recipe.
(Please note: There will be a difference of texture in the finished product).

Garam Masala: Includes only 3 spices—cinnamon, green cardamoms and cloves and the proportion to be used in these recipes is 2:2:2 unless otherwise stated. A piece of cinnamon should be approx. 1 inch long and broken into bits. *Garam masala* can be used whole or powdered as indicated.
Bay leaves used in the recipes indicate 2 or 3 leaves.

Panch Phoran: Another name in spices which is particular to Bengal. This is a mixture of equal volumes of the following five spices—*radhuni,* onion seed, aniseed, fenugreek and cummin seeds. If *radhuni* is not available, black mustard seeds are used.

Once again great stress is laid on the use of the correct amount of spices given in the ingredients for your success in cooking the Bengali way.

Baghar or, as we say in Bengal, *santhlano* or *shaumbar,* is the final addition of *ghee* or oil separately cooked with either *garam masala* or any other spices as indicated. In most cases *baghar* has not been mentioned separately but included in the recipes.

Extraction of Tamarind Juice

In a bowl add 1 cup water to a lump of tamarind—1½ inches dia. Leave for about 10 minutes and then slowly work with a spoon to extract all the pulp from the tamarind. Pass through a sieve and discard seeds and strings. For thick tamarind juice use half cup water or less as required. Any commercially prepared tamarind extract may be used.

How to make Chhana, Panir/Cottage Cheese

Boil 1 litre milk and squeeze the juice of half a lime as the milk comes to a boil. Stir, and as milk curdles, remove from fire. Strain through a muslin cloth to extract *Chhana*. Squeeze out as much of the liquid as possible and hang up or weigh down to remove the remaining moisture. One litre of milk will yield 250 grams *chhana* approximately.

How to make Doi/Dahi/Yogurt

Doi or *Dahi* takes several hours to set. I have had the best results when I have allowed it to set overnight. Boil half a litre milk for 5–10 minutes, allow it to cool until only tepid warm (blood hot). Mix in a teaspoon of *dahi* or a teaspoon of fresh lime juice stirring well so that the 'starter', as the teaspoon of *dahi* is called, is mixed in thoroughly. Pour into a suitable sized ceramic or earthen container and leave to set away from draught.

The making of *dahi* is a daily routine in most Indian homes and, therefore, a little of the *dahi* is preserved each day for a 'starter'. The *dahi* thus produced is slightly sour in taste and is the type used in the preparation of various dishes. It is also eaten sweetened with sugar as a sweet after lunch.

During winter, cover the bowl with a cloth and keep in a warm place to set (an oven may be used without heating).

Dahi can be made in a microwave oven. Warm milk to 'blood hot', add 1 tablespoon of sour dahi and mix well. Cook on low for 7 minutes. Cool.

How to prepare Coconut Milk
Break a fresh coconut in half (if you crack the coconut carefully over a bowl or glass, you can collect the coconut water which is considered very nutritious).

Grate the coconut into a bowl. Add one cup boiling water to the grated coconut, cover and leave for ten minutes. Mix the coconut and hot water well and pass through a sieve, pressing down with the back of spoon to extract all the milk. This is the *thick coconut milk*.

Return grated coconut from sieve to bowl and add one or two cups water as required in recipe. Proceed as for thick coconut milk. The second extraction is called the *thin coconut milk*.

A simpler method of extracting milk from the coconut would be to use a blender or food processor. In this method, however, *cold water* may be added to the grated coconut in the blender.

Unsweetened dessicated coconut may be used if fresh coconut is not available. 1 cup of this treated as above with warm water will give almost the same results. The addition of a little milk enhances the flavour. Coconut cream is added just after the *masala* are cooked and before the addition of water, is also a good substitute.

Glossary of Indian Words

English	Bengali	Hindi	Suggested Alternatives
Spices and Condiments			
Aniseed	Mauri	Saunf	
Asafoetida	Hing	Hing	
Bay leaves	Tej Pata	Tej Patta	
Cardamom (green)	Choto Elachi	Hara Elaychi	
Cardamom (black)	Boro Elachi	Bara Elaychi	
Carom Seeds	Jowan	Ajwain	
Chilli (red)	Sookno Lanka	Mirchi	
Cinnamon	Dalchini	Dalchini	
Cloves	Labango	Laung	
Coriander	Dhone	Dhaniya	
Cummin (white)	Shada Jeera	Jeera	
Onion Seeds	Kalo Jeera	Kalonji	
Fenugreek	Methi	Methi	
Garlic	Roshun	Lahsun	
Ginger	Ada	Adrak	
Kashmiri Chilli	Kashmiri Lanka	Rogni Mirch	Dried pimento red chillies with seeds removed. Intrinsically a chilli that colours and flavours.
Mace	Jayetri	Javitri	Peprika can also be used as a subsitute.
Mint	Pudina	Podina	
Mustard (Black & white seeds)	Sorsé	Sorson, Rai	
Nutmeg	Joiphol	Jaiphal	
Parsley	Parsley Pata	Ajmode ke patta	
Peppercorns	Gol Mirich	Kali Mirchi (Sabat)	
Pepper Powder	Golmirch Guro	Kali Mirch	
Poppy Seed	Posto	Khus Khus	
Saffron	Jaffran	Zaffran or kesar	
Rose Water	Golaper Jal	Gulab jal	
Sesame	Til	Til	
Tamarind	Tetul	Imli	
Turmeric	Holud	Haldi	
Vinegar	Sirka	Sirka	

English	Bengali	Hindi	Suggested Alternatives
Mango Ginger	Amada	Aamhaldi	
Garam masala (Mixed spices Ref: General Instruction)	Garam Masala	In a contingency substitute with crushed or ground alspice.	
Panch Phoron (5 whole spices—Ref: General Instruction)	Panch Phoran	These mixtures are typically Bengali	
Radhuni (a species of celery seeds)	Radhuni		

Fruits, Vegetables and Nuts

English	Bengali	Hindi	Suggested Alternatives
Aubergines, Eggplant or Brinjals	Begun	Baingun	
Almonds	Badam	Badam	
Banana (ripe)	Kola	Kela	
Banana (green)	Kanch Kola	Kacchha Kela	
Banana flower	Mocha	Kela ka phul	
Banana pith	Thor	Gahar	
Bitter gourd	Korola, Uchhé	Karela	
Bottle gourd, vegetable marrow	Lau	Lauki, dudhi	
Broad bean family	Sheem	Sem/papri	Mange-tout
Cabbage	Bandhakopi	Band Gobi	
Capsicum or Green peppers	Capsicum	Bara or Simla Mirch	
Carrots	Gajor	Gajar	
Cauliflower	Phulkopi	Phul gobi	
Chilli (green)	Kancha Lanka	Sabz or hari mirchi	
Climbing spinach	Pui sag	Poy Sag	Spring greens or Brussel tops
Coconut	Narkol	Nariyal	
Colacassia tuber	Kochu	Arvi	
Coriander leaves	Dhoné pata	Hara dhanya	Cilandro
Drum sticks	Sajné Danta	Shinjan	
Horse radish	Mulo	Muli	
Jackfruit (green)	Echor	Kachha Kathal	
Jackfruit (ripe)	Kanthal	Kathal	
Knol Khol	Olkopi	Ganth gobi	
Lime or Lemon	Pati Lebu	Nimbu	
Mango (green or raw)	Kacha aam	Kaccha aam, amiya/Kairi	

English	Bengali	Hindi	Suggested Alternatives
Mango (ripe)	Aam	Aam	
New Potatoes	Natun Alu	Naya Alu	
Okra or ladies finger	Dharosh	Bhindi	
Onions	Piaj	Piaz	
Papaya	Pepé	Papita	
Peas	Matarsurti	Matar ki Phaliyan/ matar	
Pistachio nut	Pesta	Pista	
Plum, dried	Alubokhara	Alubukhara	
Plum (Indian)	Topa Kool	Ber	
Parwal	Potol	Parwal	
Parwal leaves	Palta Pata	Parwal Patti	
Potato	Alu	Alu	
Pumpkin (red)	Lal kumro	Kaddu	
Pumpkin (white)	Chal Kumro	Kumhra/Petha	Marrow
Raisins	Kishmish	Kishmish	
Spinach	Palong Sag	Palak	
Spring onions	Gach Piaj	Hara Piaz	
Spring onion (Shoot with buds)	Piaj Koli		Greens of Spring Onions
Sponge gourd/ridge gourd	Jhingé	Tori, Turai	Courgettes/zuccini
Sweet potatoes	Misti Alu	Shakarkand	
Tomato	Tomato	Tamatar	
Vegetables	Tarkari, Sobji	Tarkari Sabji	
Vegetable peel	Khosha	Chhilka	
Types of edible greens, (lal sag is red in colour)	Lal sag/Noté sag	Denga Shag Patsan Shag	Spinach

Cereals and lentils:

English	Bengali	Hindi	
Rice uncooked	Chal	Chawal	
Rice cooked	Bhat	Chawal, Bhat	
Flaked Rice	Chiré	Chura	
Popped Rice	Khoi	Khoi	
Puffed Rice	Muri	Murmura/mumra	
Flour (refined)	Moida	Maida	
Flour wholemeal	Atta	Atta	
Rice flour	Sabeda	Chawal ka atta	
Semolina	Suji	Suji/Rawa	
Chick-pea flour/Bengal Gram flour	beshon	besan	

Pulses | Dal | Dal | |

| Lentils | Masur dal | Masur dal | |

English	Bengali	Hindi	Suggested Alternatives
Split black gram	Kalai dal	Urhad dal	
Spilt Bengal gram	Cholar dal	Channa dal	
Split peas	Mator dal	Mar dal	
Split green gram	Moog dal	Mung dal	
A variety of pulse	Arhor dal	Toor dal/Arhar dal	
Sun-dried small pulse cakes	Bori	Bari	

Miscellaneous

English	Bengali	Hindi
Butter	Makhon	Makkhan
Chicken	Murgi	Murgh
Yogurt unflavoured	Doi	Dahi
Egg	Dim	Anda
Fish	Maach	Machli (Machhali)
Fresh cottage cheese	Chhana	Panir
Meat	Mangsho	Gosht
Mince	Keema	Kheema
Mustard Oil	Sorsé Tel	Sorsan ka Tel
Pork	Suyorer Mangsho	Suwar ka Gosht
Sugar	Chini	Shakar, Chini

Terms of Various Fish and Sea Food   *Suggested any flaky white fish*

English	Bengali	Hindi	Suggested Alternatives
Bekti	Betki	Betki	
Cat fish (fresh water)	Magur, Shinghi	Singhara	
Climbing perch	Koi		
Crab	Kakkra	Kakkra	
Cray fish (fresh water)	Galda chingri	Bura jhinga	Small lobster
Hilsa	Elish	Palla, Bhing	Shad
Indian Salmon	Salmon	Rawas	Pacific Salmon
Prawns/Shrimps	Chingri	Jhinga	
Carp	Rui, Mrigel, Katla	Rohu	Halibut
Turtle	Ketho	Kachhua	
Mullet	Parshé	Boi	

AUNNO

CEREALS

Aunno

Cereals—Rice and Bread

Boiled rice is the staple diet of the Bengali. The more affluent eat the machine-husked, white table rice (*atap*) but the popular preference is what is commonly known as 'boiled rice'—a term used for processing the rice. The *luchi* (deep fried puffed bread made from refined wheat flour) is a speciality and is akin to the *poori*. The *porota* has been introduced to our cuisine by the Muslims. *Ghee Bhat* or the Bengali *pulau* is of a light variety and is served on special occasions.

The *khichuri* (Kedgeree) has traditionally been a dish eaten on a rainy day. In the monsoons, when the village roads are flooded and the market does not function, *khichuri*, a combination of *dal* and rice (which are always in stock at home) is eaten with boiled or fried vegetables or boiled eggs which too are readily available in the larder. Our *khichuri* is spiced and can be very tasty.

Note: Parboiled rice is manufactured by steaming the rice with the husk on. It is then dried and husked. This process pushes the vitamins and minerals to the centre of the rice and prevents the loss of these nutrients in the water. Also known as 'anti beri beri rice'.

Bhat

Boiled Rice

Two methods of cooking rice are commonly used in India: the traditional and the conservative. Bengalis use the traditional method.

Traditional Method: In a deep pan boil water equal to at least thrice the volume of rice. In the meantime, wash the rice and drain. When the water comes to a boil, add the rice and cook over medium heat till done.

Immediately drain (a small-holed colander may be used). Wash through with cold water and drain again. Return to the stove or oven to warm. Serve hot.

Nutritional Note: All nutrients including carbohydrates are drained leaving a low-calorie filler. In the case of parboiled rice, water-soluble Vitamin B is not lost.

Conservative Method: Measure out the volume of rice required. Wash well and drain dry. Using the same volume measure (e.g. cup), measure out twice the volume of water. Put rice and water in a deep pan to boil over medium heat. Half cover the pan. Cook till rice is done and all the water is absorbed. Serve hot.

Nutritional Note: All nutrients are conserved by this method including carbohydrates, providing a high calorie, rich in carbohydrate filler.

Using a Pressure/Rice Cooker: Rice can be successfully cooked in a rice-cooker following the instructions provided by the manufacturers. In a pressure-cooker, use equal volume of rice and water and cook at 15 lbs pressure for 3 minutes.

Microwave Cooking (absorption method): Wash rice, place in deep dish suitable for microwave. Add boiling water in proportion of 1 cup rice to 2 cups water. Stir in quarter teaspoon salt and half teaspoon oil or butter. Cook on high for 10 minutes. Stir, cover with tight lid and cook for 3 minutes. Remove from microwave and stand for 3 minutes and serve.

To Test if Rice is Done:

a) Insert a kitchen fork or skewer into the rice. If any grains adhere to it, the rice is done.

b) A grain of rice, pressed between thumb and finger should squash easily without any graininess.

A Few Handy Tips: Old rice increases far more in volume and absorbs much more water. One cup of rice could yield as much as 3 cups cooked rice, where the average yield is double the volume of raw rice. It is most important to adjust volume of water when using the conservative method of cooking.

- New rice tends to be sticky and yields less.
- Old rice appears to be yellowish while new rice is white (raw).
- To prevent rice from sticking, add *ghee*/butter/oil to the water while cooking. (2 teaspoons *ghee* etc. to 1 kg rice).

Note: 'American Wild Rice' has no relation to the rice grown in India.

Bahu Khuda

The Hungry Bride's Pilaff

Traditionally it was one of the many duties of the *Bahu* (daughter-in-law) to serve the family members and only after everyone had eaten, did she sit down to her meal. Often, one or more of the items on the menu were finished. One such *Bahu* was not going to be deprived of Pilaff, a favourite dish, and invented this tasty recipe which could be cooked quickly with readily available ingredients.

Bahu Khuda (Bahu = bride, Khuda = hunger), a favourite recipe of the late Mrs.C.R.Das, has been contributed by her daughter, late Mrs. Bhaskar Mukerji.

250 gms mustard oil
300 gms onions, peeled, halved
   and sliced finely
1 kg rice (polished, small-grained)
   washed and dried, mixed with
   ½ teaspoon turmeric powder
100 gms onions, peeled, halved
   and sliced finely
10 green chillies, picked and slit
   (more or less may be added)
½ teaspoon turmeric powder
1 teaspoon salt
hot water*

*Notes:
(a) Pressure Cooking: equal
   volume of water to rice.
(b) Conservative Method: double
   volume of water to rice.
(c) Microwave: Follow recipe as
   above Add 1½ volumes of hot
   water to rice stir in green chil-
   lics and salt, pour into
   suitable dish to microwave.
   Cook uncovered on high for 8
   mins. Cook covered for another
   6 mins on medium and let it
   stand for 4 mins and serve.

Heat oil to smoking point. Fry 300 gms onion to golden brown, drain and set aside.

Add the rice (prepared with turmeric) and 100 gms sliced onions to the remaining oil. Stir-fry for several minutes till the rice changes colour.

Add half teaspoon turmeric and continue frying till the oil comes to the surface.

Mix in the previously browned onions to the rice, and fry for another 5–7 minutes.

Add the hot water.

Stir in the green chillies and salt.

Cover and cook till done.

A good accompaniment with: *Bhaja, Curry* or *any gravy dish.*

Serves: 8–10

Ghee Bhat

Bengali Rice Pilaff

1 kg fine long grained rice
   (preferably basmati), washed
   and dried
250 gms ghee
30 gms raisins, picked, washed
   and soaked in water to soften
1 teaspoon salt
3 bay leaves*
4 inches cinnamon*
4 cardomoms*
6 cloves*
250 gms. onions, peeled, halved
   and sliced thinly. Fry till crisp
   and golden brown. Drain and
   set aside.

* garam masala

Measure rice in cupfuls. Using the same measure, pour double the measure of water to rice in a large pan and set to boil.

When water comes to a boil, add the rice, stir and half cover, and let cook on medium flame till rice is done. (approximately 15–20 mins.)

Immediately wash out rice with cold water to remove starch. Drain thoroughly.

Heat *ghee* in a separate pan. Fry all the *garam masala* till they start to splutter.

Stir in rice using a skewer. Fry till the rice starts to brown.

Stir in salt and raisins and cook for a few minutes more.

Sprinkle with previously browned onions and serve immediately

Variation I:
Same as above. Omit onions.

In a large pan, heat quarter of the *ghee*. Add rice and sauté till brown. Add water and cook as above following instructions for "Stir in Salt" to end.

Variation II:
Same as above. Omit onions and raisins. Butter may be substituted for *ghee*.

Follow instructions up to ". . . Drain thoroughly". Return rice to pan. Add butter. Stir for a few minutes with a skewer. Serve immediately.

Variation III
Same as above. Omit onions.

Additional requirement: 250 ml. (1 cup) milk.

Follow instructions till ". . . Stir in rice" but only *half cook* the rice. In a pan heat the *ghee*. Fry the *garam masala* till they splutter. Stir in the rice and sauté till brown.

Add the milk, salt and raisins. Stir, cover and simmer till done. If the rice remains uncooked and the milk dries up, sprinkle water, cover and cook till tender.

A good accompaniment with: *Curries*

Serves: 8–10

Khichuri

Kedegree

Khichuri has traditionally been a dish eaten on a rainy day. A Bengali housewife looks at the sky and decides the menu is *khichuri*, *bhaja* and *bharta* with generous dollops of *ghee*.

During the monsoons, when village roads could be flooded in a heavy downpour and markets cease to function, the *khichuri*, a combination of rice and *dal* which are always in stock at home is eaten along with boiled or fried vegetables or boiled eggs, *bhaja*, *bharta* or *bhat*.

Khichuri can be made with or without vegetables. It can be mild or spicy. For infants and invalids, a mild *khichuri* of a soupy consistency is served. For special occasions it can be enriched by first frying the *dal* and rice.

Khichuri means a mixture. You can make it anyway you like. I am giving you my family's favourite recipe.

250 gms rice*
250 gms roasted mung dal*
250 gms cauliflower, broken into
    large flowerets.
100 gms peas, shelled
200 gms potatoes, cut into
    quarters
100 gms small onions (pearl
    onions), peeled, whole
6 green chillies, picked and slit
1/2 teaspoon turmeric powder
2 teaspoons cummin powder
1/2 teaspoon chilli powder
1/2 teaspoon coriander powder
    (optional)**
1 teaspoon ginger paste
    (optional)**
1/2 teaspoon sugar
1 1/2 teaspoons salt
1–1 1/2 litres water (approx 6 cups).

*washed separately, drained and
    half dried.
**mix into a thick paste with
    water

Bring the water to a boil in a large, deep pan.

Add the rice and *dal* to the boiling water and allow to cook till rice is half cooked.

Stir in *masala* pastes, salt and sugar. Simmer for 5–7 minutes.

Add the vegetables and green chillies and continue to simmer till they are cooked. By this time, both rice and *dal* will be cooked as well.

To make the *Shaumbar*: Heat the *ghee* in a frying pan. Sauté red chillies, *garam masala* and bay leaves for 1 minute.

Add the sliced onions and fry till golden brown.

Stir in the *ghee-masala*-onion mixture into the cooked *khichuri*. Season if required. Stir and remove from heat. Serve hot. Melted, hot *ghee* poured over the *khichuri* enhances the flavour.

Making *khichuri* by the pressure cooking method: Put all the ingredients except the *shaumbar* into the pressure cooker. Add approximately 750 ml water (water should be one inch above the ingredient level). Cook at 15 lbs pressure for 3 minutes. Stir in the *ghee-masala*-onion paste and proceed as directed above.

For the Shaumbar
150 gms ghee
100 gms onions, peeled, halved
    and sliced finely.
4 bay leaves
4 dry red chillies
4 inch cinnamon stick, broken
    into 4 pieces
4 green cardamoms*
6 cloves*

*garam masala

A good accompaniment with: *Bhaja, bhorta, bhaté.* Hilsa fish *bhaja* is served on special occasions. *Ghee* is always poured over individual portions. A variety of pickles is also served.

Note: Please note normally *garama masala* consists of 2: 2: 2: cinnamon, cardamoms, cloves

Serves: 10–12

Luchi

Deep fried Puffed Bread

250 gms flour
½ tablespoon ghee
a pinch of salt
water as required
ghee for deep frying luchis

Sieve the flour and salt. Add *ghee* and sufficient water to bind and knead into a soft pliable dough. The kneading of the dough is most important for success in making puffed *luchis*.

Divide into 32 small balls and roll on floured board into rounds of approximately 4-inch diameter as thinly and evenly as possible.

Deep fry one at a time in *karai*, pressing the centre of the *luchi* gently with a slotted spoon until *luchi* puffs up. Fry for a minute, turn and fry the other side for another minute. Using a slotted spoon remove *luchi* from pan, draining off *ghee*.

Note: The temperature of the *ghee* is very important. It should be heated to smoking and then allowed to simmer at a constant medium hot temperature. The *luchis* will not puff up if the *ghee* is either too hot or not hot enough.

The above quantity of flour will make approximately 32 *luchis*.

A good accompaniment with: *Dal, Alurdom, any fish* or *meat curry*

Serves 6–8

Porota

500 gms flour
2 tablespoons ghee
a pinch salt
a pinch bicarbonate soda
1 tablespoon dahi
1 cup water approx
ghee to smear on porotas,
    ghee for frying porotas

Sieve flour and salt together.

Mix in bicarbonate of soda. Rub in *ghee* and *dahi*. Add water and form into dough. Knead dough until soft and pliable—at least 20 minutes.

Divide into 8 equal portions.

On a floured board, roll dough into a large round. Smear or brush with melted *ghee*. Lightly roll from one edge to the other. With the two ends roll in opposite direction until they converge to form an *S*. Fold one half of the *S* over the other. Press down with the palm of the hand.

Roll out again on floured board to a diameter of at least 8 inches.

Heat some *ghee* in a fry pan and fry *porota* in gently simmering *ghee* until lightly browned on both sides. Drain well before serving.

A good accompaniment with: *Dal, meat, some fish recipes.*

Serves: 4–8

Radhaballobhi Luchi

Stuffed Luchis

For the Dough:
500 gms flour
1/2 teaspoon salt
2 tablespoons ghee
1 cup water approx

For Filling:
4 tablespoons kalai or urhad dal
*   soaked in water overnight or*
*   for several hours*
1/2 teaspoon aniseed*
1/2 teaspoon cummin seed*
1/8 teaspoon onion seeds*
1/2 teaspoon salt
a pinch sugar
2 tablespoons ghee
ghee for frying radhaballobhis

*dry-fried and powdered

To prepare filling, drain water from *dal*. Grind to a fine paste. Heat one tablespoon *ghee* in a *karai*, add *dal*, the powdered *masalas*, salt and sugar. Stir and cook till completely blended. Keep aside until dough is ready.

To prepare dough, sieve together the flour and salt. Add one tablespoon of *ghee* and sufficient water to form pliable dough. Knead until soft.

Divide dough into 8 portions and roll into balls.

Inserting finger in the centre of a ball of dough, work with fingers to increase the hole to form a cup.

Stuff the dough cup with some of the filling. Close cup, sealing well, re-roll to a ball. Press flat and then roll on floured board into rounds twice the size of ordinary *luchis* but much thicker.

Deep fry in *ghee* till lightly browned. Drain off *ghee* and serve.

Note: Care must be taken when rolling the *radhaballobhis* to ensure that the surface dough does not break under pressure from the roller.

A good accompaniment with: *Dry Alurdom* or *Dal*

Serves: 8

DAL

LENTILS

Dal

Pulses & Legumes

Dal is always served at a Bengali meal. This is a soupy preparation made from pulses or legumes. It is a readily available and an inexpensive source of protein. Many different types of *dal* and methods of cooking exist and I have tried to give a representative selection. Prepared with care and imagination, a *dal* dish can be very tasty and I have seen many of my friends, Indians and foreigners, going through an entire dinner with only *dal-bhat* and *luchis* in preference to the more exotic fish and meat preparations.

Basically, *dal* is boiled with water and can be seasoned with a variety of spices. Different combinations of spices will completely alter the taste of a *dal*.

In this section, I have included a few preparations with *dal* such as *Dhokar Dalna, Dal Chenchki* etc., which are in fact served in lieu of a vegetable dish and in addition to a normal *dal*.

Toor Dal with Vegetables

250 gms aurhor dal
2 cupfuls of mixed vegetables cut
in 1 inch cubes or lengthwise
(vegetables such as cauliflower,
horse radish, marrow, parwal,
flat beans, potatoes, drum
sticks and peas can all be
used or any combination of the
above).
a small bunch of coriander
leaves, picked clean
6–8 cups water
1 teaspoon turmeric paste
1/4 teaspoon chilli paste
1 tablespoon coriander paste
2 tablespoons cummin paste
1 tablespoon ginger paste
6–8 green chillies, slit
salt to taste
1/2 tablespoon sugar
1 tablespoon ghee
1/2 teaspoon panch phoran

Wash *dal* and add to boiling water in *dekchi*.

Stir. When *dal* comes to a boil, add vegetables such as potatoes and horse radish, which take longer to cook. Add turmeric and chilli paste. Mix well and simmer over medium fire.

Add vegetables to *dal* according to their cooking time, estimating that the *dal* will take approximately half an hour to cook. Finally add the coriander, cummin and ginger pastes, slit green chillies, salt and sugar. Mix thoroughly and simmer another 10 minutes or till *dal* and vegetables are cooked.

In a *karai*, heat the *ghee*, add *panch phoran*. When this stops spluttering, pour into the *dal*. Stir, bring to a boil and remove from fire.

A good accompaniment with: *Rice* or *Ghee Bhat*

Serves: 6–8

Cholar Dal

Channa Dal

250 gms cholar or channa dal
4–6 cups water
1 teaspoon turmeric paste
¼ – ½ teaspoon chilli paste
1 tablespoon coriander paste
2 tablespoons cummin paste
1 tablespoon garam masala paste
4–8 green chillies, slit
¼ of a coconut, diced very fine
   and fried in ghee till browned
1 tablespoon ghee
1 tablespoon raisins, soaked in
   water, dried and fried
3 bay leaves
salt to taste
2–4 teaspoons sugar
garam masala (see page 7)

Wash the *dal*.

Boil water in a *dekchi* and when bubbling, add the *dal*. Add the turmeric and chilli pastes and stir. Continue simmering over medium heat until *dal* is nearly done.

Add the coriander, cummin, *garam masala* pastes and green chillies. Also add salt and sugar to taste.

Mix well and continue cooking until *dal* is soft and thick.

In a separate *dekchi* or *karai*, heat the *ghee*. Add bay leaves and *garam masala*. When spluttering stops, pour over *dal* and mix thoroughly.

Finally add fried diced coconut. Stir and remove from fire.

Note: Traditionally *Cholar Dal* is sweetened more than other *dals* and served with *Luchi*.

A good accompaniment with: *Luchi, Porota* or *Ghee Bhat*

Serves: 6

Dal Chenchki

250 gms masur dal
125 gms or half cup oil
½ tsp turmeric paste
1 teaspoon chilli paste, or more
1 large onion, halved and sliced
  fine
10–12 small pearl onions, peeled
1 tablespoon ghee
garam masala (see page 7)

Soak dal in water for half an hour. Drain. Then wash dal thoroughly in several changes of water. Spread dal thinly over a large thali or plate and leave until half-dry.

In a karai or pan heat the oil. Add the sliced onions and fry till lightly browned. Add turmeric and chilli paste. Fry for a few minutes and then add dal. Stir well.

Fry the dal over a medium fire stirring continually. When dal begins to change colour, add the pearl onions and continue frying.

Keep handy approximately 2 cups water and sprinkle a very little at a time over the dal so that it does not catch at the bottom of the pan. Add salt and sugar to taste.

Continue frying the dal, sprinkling water a little at a time, as required, so that finally the dal is cooked but still remains whole and there is practically no gravy. The dal is done when it mashes easily between a finger and thumb. Remove from fire.

In a dekchi heat the ghee and then add the garam masala. As soon as the garam masala stops spluttering, pour over dal, stirring thoroughly.

Reheat over a very gentle fire, if necessary.

Note: Caution is necessary when adding water because if too much water is added, the dal becomes a lump. The dal in chenchki must be soft to the touch but remain whole.

A good accompaniment with: Rice or Luchi

Serves: 4–6

Dhokar Dalna

Fried Channa Dal Cubes with Gravy

For the Dhoka:
250 gms channa/cholar dal
1 teaspoon ginger paste
¼ teaspoon turmeric paste
¼ teaspoon chilli paste
1 onion halved and sliced fine
1 teaspoon salt
3 tablespoons ghee
6–8 tablespoons ghee or oil

For the Dalna:
3–4 potatoes (optional, each cut in
* 6 pieces)*
1 onion, ground to a paste
1 tablespoon turmeric paste
1–1½ teaspoons chilli paste,
* salt and sugar to taste*
2 tablespoons ghee
4 cups water
2 bay leaves
* garam masala (see page 7)*

To make the *dhoka*, soak the *channa dal* in water overnight. In the morning drain and grind to a fine paste.

Heat 3 tablespoons *ghee* in a *karai* and fry the sliced onions till brown and crisp. Remove from *karai*. In the remaining *ghee* add the turmeric, chilli and ginger pastes. Fry for a couple of minutes.

Add the *channa dal* paste and keep stirring and frying until the greater part of the moisture from the *channa dal* paste has evaporated.

Add the browned onions and salt to taste. Mix thoroughly and continue frying, stirring all the while for another 5 minutes. By this time, the *channa dal* paste should be well fried and all the *ghee* in the pan will have been absorbed into the paste—which should still be soft but should stick together in a lump or ball.

Place the fried *channa dal* paste on a *thala* or plate with a slightly raised edge and smooth down evenly to half inch thickness. While still hot, mark and cut diagonally crosswise into medium sized diamond-shaped pieces. Leave to cool and set for 20 minutes.

Heat the 6–8 tablespoons *ghee* or oil in a *karai* or pan. Fry the diamond-shaped pieces of *channa dal* or *dhoka*, a few at a time, until lightly browned. Remove from pan with slotted spoon draining off as much *ghee* as possible.

If oil has been used for frying, keep aside for other use. If *ghee* is used, measure 2 tablespoons and use for cooking *dalna*.

Lightly fry the potatoes in hot *ghee* and keep aside.

Add the bay leaves and *garam masala*. Fry for a couple of minutes and add the *masala* pastes, salt and sugar to taste. Fry for several minutes or until *masalas* changes colour. Add 4 cups water. Stir and add the fried potatoes. Simmer over medium heat until potatoes are three-quarters done.

Add the *dhoka* to the *karai*. Place the *dhoka* so that it cooks in the *karai* in a single layer. Shake *karai* from time to time, spooning gravy over *dhoka*. Continue cooking until gravy is half the original quantity of water added. Remove from fire.

Note: Dhoka absorbs liquid even after being removed from the fire and gravy must be left accordingly.

A good accompaniment with: *Rice* and *Luchi*

Serves: 4–6

Ghugni

Whole Chick-peas in Masala

500 gms Kabuli channa/chick-
  peas
125 gms potatoes, peeled and
  diced into ¼-inch cubes
125 gms ghee
1 teaspoon whole black pepper
1 teaspoon whole coriander seeds
1 teaspoon cummin seeds
½ teaspoon turmeric powder
1 coconut, finely diced
⅛ teaspoon aniseed
2 or 3 dry red chillies, whole
2–3 cups water
a 2-inch piece ginger cut into fine
  sticks
4 bay leaves*
3 cardamoms green*
4 inch stick cinnamon broken into
  bits*
6 cloves*

*garam masala

Soak chick-peas in water for 5–6 hours or overnight.

Drain and put to boil in water to cover until chick-peas are done. (Chick-peas may be pressure cooked for 20 minutes).

Remove from fire, cool and then gently rub chick-peas between palms of the hands to remove skin. The skin will float to the top. Remove by draining off water.

Heat a *tawa* and dry-fry the *garam masala*, black pepper, coriander and cummin for a few minutes till roasted. Remove from *tawa* and grind to a fine powder.

Heat all but one tablespoon *ghee* in a *karai* and separately fry the diced potatoes and finely diced coconut until just brown.

Then add the chick-peas. Stir in and continue cooking for about 5 minutes.

Add the mixed powdered *masala* and the turmeric and continue frying for another 5–7 minutes.

Add the water and salt to taste.

Continue cooking until nearly all the water is absorbed.

In a *karai* heat the remaining *ghee*. Add the red chillies broken in half and the aniseed and cook until they stop spluttering. Pour over the chick-peas and mix well.

Add the ginger sticks and stir again.

Serve hot.

May be served by itself as a snack or *with Luchi* or *Radhaballabhi Luchi*

Serves: 8–10

Kalai Dal

Urhad Dal

250 gms kalai dal/urhad dal
6 cups water
¼ teaspoon turmeric paste or
    pinch powdered turmeric
2 tablespoons ginger paste
salt and sugar to taste
1 teaspoon ghee
½ teaspoon mustard seeds
2 whole dry red chillies

Wash *dal* thoroughly and add to boiling water. Add the turmeric. Cook over brisk fire until done.

Add the ginger paste and mix thoroughly. At the same time, add salt to taste and very little sugar.

Heat *ghee* in *karai*, add mustard seeds and dry red chillies and when this stops spluttering, pour over *dal*. Mix well.

This preparation of *kalai dal* is delightful on a hot summer's day served at room temperature.

A good accompaniment with: *Rice*

Serves: 4–6

Bhaja and Bharta

Monama

Shukto

Musur and Cholar Dal

Tomato Farci

Matarsutir Dal

Green Pea Dal

1 kg green peas, shelled
125 gms ghee
1 tablespoon turmeric paste
1½ teaspoons chilli paste
2 tablespoons ginger paste
2 tablespoons coriander paste
1 teaspoon black pepper,
   powdered or pasted
1 teaspoon cummin paste
3–4 bay leaves
salt and sugar to taste
*garam masala (see page 7)
3 bay leaves

The Preparation:
Before the green pea *dal* can be cooked, the outer skin of the green pea has to be removed.

Mix in 2 or 3 tablespoons of coarse salt or rock salt with the shelled peas. Leave for 20 minutes to half an hour.

Then rub the peas between the palms of your hands and the skin will come off.

Transfer peas to a large bowl of water and continue rubbing and mixing the peas with your hands. The outer skin of the peas will float to the top of the water.

Carefully drain off the water, removing skins with it.

Wash peas again and drain.

The Cooking:
In a *dekchi* heat all but 1 tablespoon of the *ghee*. When hot, add the peas and fry until just turning brown.

Add the *masala* pastes and cook, stirring continuously.

After about 5 minutes add the water. Bring to the boil and cook until peas are very soft, but not disintegrating.

Add salt and sugar to taste.

In another pan or *karai*, heat the remaining 1 tablespoon *ghee*. Add bay leaves and *garam masala* and when spluttering stops, add the green pea *dal*.

Stir well, bring to the boil, cook for 5 minutes and remove from fire.

A good accompaniment with: *Rice, Luchi* or *Porota*

Serves: 8–10

Misti Sona Moog Dal

Sweetened Mung Dal

250 gms sona mung dal
12 small whole pearl onions
6–8 green chillies, slit
½ cup milk
1–2 teaspoons sugar
salt to taste
1 tablespoon ghee
4 bay leaves
½ teaspoon whole cummin seeds

In a medium hot *karai* dry roast *mung dal* till delicately brown and aromatic.

Wash and put the *mung dal* to boil.

After 10 minutes add the pearl onions, green chillies and salt.

Simmer until *dal* is cooked.

In a separate pan, heat *ghee* and fry the bay leaves and cummin seeds for a few minutes. Pour in the cooked *dal* and simmer for 5 minutes.

Add ½ cup milk and sugar.

Adjust seasoning and remove from fire.

Variation I:
Add 2 *tablespoons cummin paste* along with the other ground spices. In the *ghee*, along with bay leaves and cummin seeds, add 2 *tablespoons aam aada* (a root that resembles ginger and fresh turmeric but has an aroma of raw mango. Also known as *ambé halad* in some region.)

Variation II:
Add fresh 6 young *parwal*, peeled and halved to the *mung dal* along with 12 pearl onions.

Variation III:
Mung dal can also be made with plain *mung dal* (not roasted). Omit milk and sugar.

Note: Sona Moog is a variety of small grained fried *mung dal* available in Bengal. Small grained *mung* fried on a *tawa* may be substituted. Alternatively, this recipe can also be made with ordinary *mung dal*.

A good accompaniment with: *Rice* or *Luchi*

Serves: 8–10

Muro Dal

Fish Head cooked with Dal

½ kg mung dal
250–300 gms (approx) fish head
 either rahu, rawas or bekti,
 cleaned
1 tablespoon turmeric paste
1 tablespoon coriander paste
1½ tablespoons cummin paste
1–2 teaspoons chilli paste
6–7 green chillies
½ teaspoon panch phoran
1 tablespoon oil or ghee
salt and sugar to taste
oil for frying fish head
6 cups of water
*1 tablespoon garam masala paste
 *(3 bay leaves, 2 green
 cardamoms, 2 cloves, 2 inch
 cinnamon ground to a paste
 with water)

In a medium hot karai, dry roast mung dal till delicately brown and aromatic.

Wash the mung dal thoroughly and boil in 6 cups of water.

Add the turmeric and chilli powder and salt to taste and continue simmering until dal is more than half done.

In the meantime, in another pan fry the cleaned fish head till quite brown, then break into pieces.

Add the pieces of fish head and green chillies to dal and at the same time add the coriander and cummin paste. Continue cooking until spices are well blended and the dal is cooked.

In a separate pan heat 1 tablespoon ghee and the panch phoran and fry until it begins to splutter. Pour this over the hot dal, stir and continue cooking for a couple of minutes. Stir in sugar to taste.

Then add garam masala paste and cook 2 minutes longer.

Remove from fire.

A good accompaniment with: Rice or Luchi

Serves: 4–6

Musur Dal

Lentils

250 gms musur dal
3 cups water or more
1 teaspoon turmeric paste
a pinch of chilli paste
4–6 green chilies (optional)
1 teaspoon ghee
3–4 whole dry red chillies
1/4 teaspoon panch phoran
salt to taste

Wash the *dal*.

In the meantime, set 4 cups of water to boil in a *dekchi*.

As soon as water begins to bubble, add *dal*. Stir.

Then add the turmeric and chilli paste, and the green chillies, if desired.

Continue cooking until *dal* is soft but there is still plenty of gravy.

At this stage, in a separate *karai*, heat a teaspoon of *ghee* and fry the *panch phoran* and red chillies until spluttering stops.

Pour over *dal* and mix well.

Add salt to taste, stir well and then remove from fire.

Note: Musur dal is eaten most often with everyday meals as it is very nutritious and light.

A good accompaniment with: *Rice*

Serves: 6

Tauk Dal

Sweet-sour Dal

250 gms arhar dal
4 cups water
4 medium sized green mangoes,
    peeled and cut into 6/8 pieces
    each lengthwise
1 teaspoon turmeric
1/2 teaspoon onion seeds
4–6 green chillies, slit
salt to taste
1–2 teaspoons sugar or to taste
1 teasopoon ghee

Wash *dal* and stir into boiling water.

Add turmeric and after stirring again, continue cooking for about 20 minutes.

Add the green mangoes, green chillies and salt to taste.

Continue cooking until green mangoes are soft but not mushy.

Add sugar to taste.

In a *karai* heat *ghee* and add onion seeds. Cook until onion seeds stop spluttering and pour over *dal*. Stir well. Bring to the boil once and remove from fire.

This *dal* tastes best served at room temperature.

A good accompaniment with: *Rice*

Serves: 6

TARKARI

VEGETABLES

Tarkari

Vegetables

It may be of interest to know that while Bengalis are known to be primarily fish eaters, they are also very fond of vegetable preparations and will eat all types of vegetables.

It is necessary to mention here the important part played by the widows of Bengal in the development of vegetarian cooking. The Hindu code deemed that widows were strictly vegetarian and in orthodox homes even the use of onions and garlic was forbidden to them. The kitchen for widows was totally separate from that for the rest of the family and they always cooked for themselves. There were strict rituals to be followed with regard to bathing and religious rites before cooking, and they ate on their own within their kitchen confines. No non-vegetarian was permitted anywhere near the widows' kitchens. Much of our vegetarian cuisine owes thanks to these widows who, in their search for variety within such limitations, have shown great ingenuity and versatility and have indeed given us a wealth of vegetable preparations.

I have made particular mention later on about the banana plant and how Bengalis use each and every portion of that plant. Historically, every village home had banana trees. They just grew. Some of the fruit were not of good enough quality to be eaten ripe, and recipes were innovated to make delicate preparations with the green bananas, the flower and the pith.

The succulent leaves and stems of creepers of various members of the gourd family and other greens growing around the village home, have always found a place in a Bengali dish. In fact, the ability to mix different available vegetables and create delicate new dishes expresses the art of Bengali cooking. In Bengali, we refer to all these as *danta* (stem) or *sag* (leaves) which includes spinach. I have not given recipes for all such preparations but an adventurous cook can always substitute a different *sag* to that mentioned in the recipe.

The recipes have been given in the order they are normally served—the *bhajas* followed by *bhaté, pora, bora, chenchki, ghanto, chorchori, sorsé, dalna* and *dolma* to enable the reader to pick out with greater ease the type of preparation and the vegetable to be included in the menu.

Shukto

Mixed bitter-sweet Vegetables

2 medium sized potatoes
1 medium sized brinjal
1 horse radish
1 green banana
4 parwals
3 sajné-danta or drumsticks
a bunch palta pata (leaves of the
    parwal plant or 2 korolas or
    bitter gourd)
a pinch ground turmeric paste
1 tablespoon ground ginger paste
1 tablespoon ground cummin paste
1 teaspoon ground mustard paste
salt to taste
6 medium sized boris (optional)
2 tablespoons oil
2–3 cups water
1 tablespoon ghee
a pinch panch phoran
1–2 tablespoons milk
1–2 teaspoons sugar

Peel and cut the potatoes in half lengthwise and then crosswise on the bias into quarter inch slices.

Slit the brinjal in four lengthwise and then crosswise into half inch thick slices.

Slit the horse radish in four and then cut on the bias into 1 inch length.

Trim and scrape the *parwals*. Cut in half lengthwise and cut in 4 pieces on the bias.

Trim *sajné-danta* and cut in 2 inch lengths.

Halve *korola* and slice finely or use 8–10 *palta pata* (the last gives the bitter taste to *shukto*).

Fry the *boris* in hot oil and keep aside.

Fry the *palta* or *korola*.

Add all the other vegetables and fry for a few minutes until lightly browned.

Add all the *masalas* and mix thoroughly with vegetables.

Add salt and finally two cups of water. Continue simmering until vegetables are all cooked.

Heat teaspoon of *ghee* in another pan.

Add a pinch of *panch phoran*. Fry till spluttering stops and pour this over the simmering vegetables. Mix thoroughly. Add a tablespoon of milk and a teaspoon of sugar. Simmer for five minutes and remove from fire.

Note: Shukto begins the afternoon meal (especially in summers).

A good accompaniment with: *Rice*

Serves: 6–8

Bhaja
Fries

Bhaja is always served with *dal* and rice at a traditional meal. It is either *maach bhaja* (fried fish) or a vegetable *bhaja*.

Every vegetable lends itself to this form of cooking. Often the vegetable is first picked, washed, sliced and fried. Or it is combined with another vegetable or sliced onions to vary the flavour.

Nutritionally, these vegetables retain most of their values as the goodness is sealed in by frying. However, they become high calorie foods after frying.

Begun Bhaja
Fried Brinjal

Brinjal, salt, turmeric, mustard oil for frying.

Cut brinjal into quarter inch rounds or quarter lengthwise. Rub in turmeric and salt. Deep fry till tender.

Alu Bhaja
Fried Potatoes

Large potatoes, salt, turmeric, and oil for frying.

Scrub potatoes and peel if desired. Cut into one-eighth inch rounds and keep soaked in water till required. Drain. Rub in salt and turmeric and fry till tender or crisp.

Khosha Bhaja
Dry-fried Vegetable Peels

2 cups peel from bottle gourd, pumpkin and potatoes, washed thoroughly and cut in fine julienne
1 onion, halved and sliced very fine
½ teaspoon turmeric paste (optional)
2 tablespoons oil
¼ teaspoon mustard seeds

Heat oil in pan. Add mustard seeds. Cook until it stops spluttering.

Add the *masala*, julienned peel and the onions. Continue frying until onions become soft and the peel is cooked. If too dry while cooking, sprinkle water as and when necessary.

A good accompaniment with: *Rice*

Serves: 4

Beshon Bhaja

Vegetables fried in Chick-pea flour batter

1 cup besan or chick-pea flour
1 teaspoon oil
250 ml water (as required)
1 teaspoon chilli powder (or to
*   taste)*
salt to taste
oil for deep frying
a pinch of baking soda (optional),
*   improves the flavour*

Pour *besan* into a large bowl and add 1 teaspoon oil. Mix thoroughly. Add water to make batter (the consistency should be thick enough to coat vegetable thinly). Add all the other ingredients and salt to taste. Whip batter well and set aside for half an hour.

To test batter: Drop a little into a bowl of water. It will float but be partly submerged. If it sinks it should be further whipped. Over beating (when it floats totally) produces a honey comb texture and absorbs excessive oil.

Dip the prepared vegetables in this batter coating well. Heat oil to very hot, then reduce to a simmer. Fry the vegetables in batter in this oil until a rich brown. Remove from pan with slotted spoon. Drain extra oil on absorbent paper and serve. The above quantity of batter will coat approx. half a kg of vegetables.

NUTRITIONAL NOTE: Besan adds protein value to the *bhaja*. However, all *bhajas* have high calorific value.

Following are some of the vegetables which may be fried in this manner:

1. *Onions:* Use large sized onions. Cut into thin rounds. Coat with batter and fry.
2. *Red Pumpkin:* Slice one-eighth inch thick. Coat with batter and fry.
3. *Cucumber:* Slice into rounds. Coat with batter and fry.
4. *Brinjal (Begun):* Cut lengthwise, then slice one-eighth inch thick. Coat with batter and fry. Add 1 teaspoon poppy seeds or quarter teaspoon onion seed or aniseed to the batter.
5. *Cauliflower:* Cut in medium flowerets. Coat well and fry.
6. *Potatoes:* Slices into thin rounds. Coat in batter and fry.
7. *Parwals:* Peeled, cut in half lengthwise. Coat in batter and fry.
8. *Sweet Potatoes:* First boil, then slice as fine as possible. Coat in batter and fry.
9. *Green Chillies:* Use the large, not very hot, green chillies. Coat with batter and fry.
10. *Capsicum:* Cut in 1 inch strips. Coat with batter and fry.
11. *Spinach:* Use only fresh young leaves. Remove stems. Coat each leaf separately with batter and fry.
12. *Bangla Paan:* Take small paan leaves, or halve large ones. Coat in batter and fry.
13. *Zucchini:* Slice thinly into rounds. Coat in batter and fry.

Onions fried in *besan* batter are commonly called *Piaji* and brinjals fried in this manner are called *Benguni*. The others are classified under *Beshon Bhaja*, except *Phuluri*—a speciality.

Phuluri

1 cup thinly sliced onion halves
4 tablespoons besan or gram flour
6 tablespoons water
1/4 teaspoon chilli powder
2 green chillies, chopped fine
1/4 tsp Bicarbonate of soda
    (optional)
salt to taste
oil for deep frying

Make a thick batter or paste with the *besan* and water. Whip in chilli powder, and salt to taste and green chillies if preferred. Add separated onion slices. Mix well. Heat oil in pan to smoking hot, then reduce heat to medium, simmer and deep fry onion mixture by the tablespoon until *phuluri* is crisply brown. Remove with slotted spoon, drain off oil. Serve hot.

Variation: Shrimps added to the above make delightful *bhajas*.

Can be served as a snack also.

Serves: 4–6

Bhaté, Pora and Bharta
Boiled or Roasted Vegetables

Bhaté is merely boiled vegetables mashed and mixed with salt, mustard oil, chopped onions and green chillies.

The vegetable is boiled in the same water in which the rice is cooking and thereby derives the name (*bhat:* cooked rice). It is popular with the Bengali housewife as it is quick and economical to prepare.

In Bengal, all varieties of fresh vegetables are used for making *bhaté*. The vegetables are cut in large chunks or kept whole, as necessary, and slipped into boiling rice and cooked with it. It is removed after the water is drained from the rice. Sometimes when the vegetable is small or is required to be chopped fine, a muslin bag is used. The vegetables are put inside a muslin bag which is loosely tied and then immersed in boiling rice.

Pora is roasted on an open fire or baked in an oven. It is peeled after roasting.

Bhaté or *pora* is normally eaten as an accompaniment to rice and *dal*.

The basic ingredients for *bhaté* or *pora* are essentially a little salt and mustard oil mixed in with the boiled vegetables. Onions and green chillies are added in some cases as also freshly made mustard paste to improve the flavour.

On occasions when there has been a bereavement in the family and no cooking is done other than to boil rice, *bhaté* is normally eaten without the addition of either onion, chilli or salt.

For those who find the taste of mustard oil too strong, butter or *ghee* may be substituted or any other oil. But in the case of the latter, it must be cooked to smoking hot and then added to the vegetable while still warm.

Finally, *bhaté* can of course be made separately by boiling the vegetables in a pan of water till done.

Sometimes, as a variation to the taste of *bhaté*, I use the oil from a bottle of mango pickle or any other spiced sour hot relish or pickle. I also chop in a little of the pickle and add to the *bhaté*. It has a delightful taste.

Alu Bhaté

Mashed Potato

2 large potatoes
2 tablespoons mustard oil
1/4 onion, finely chopped
1/2 teaspoon salt
1 green chilli, finely chopped

Boil 2 large potatoes until well done and soft to the touch.

Mash. Add 2 tablespoons mustard oil or more if preferred, salt, onion and green chilli. Mix well. Shape into a mound and serve on a small plate or make an individual ball for each person.

Kumro Bhaté

Boiled Red Pumpkin

1/2 kg. red pumpkin
1 tablespoon mustard paste
1 onion, finely chopped
3–4 green chillies, chopped fine
2–3 green limes, juiced
a pinch of sugar (optional)
1–2 tablespoons mustard oil
salt to taste.

Boil and drain the pumpkin, mash well. Mix in the mustard paste, oil, onions, green chillies and lime juice to the pumpkin mixture. Add a little sugar and salt to taste. Mix thoroughly and serve cold.

A good accompaniment with: *Rice*

Serves: 6

Begun Pora

Roasted Brinjal

1 large brinjal
½ onion, chopped fine
3 tablespoons mustard oil
1 green chilli, chopped fine
½ teaspoon salt, or more to taste

Take a large brinjal and brush some mustard oil over it. Roast over live coals or in a hot oven until the skin of the brinjal is scorched and brown and peels off easily. Peel skin off the roasted brinjal and mash to a pulp.

Mix the onion, mustard oil, green chilli and salt with the mashed brinjal and serve.

Variation
As a change, 2 tablespoons unsweetened *dahi* can be added.

COMBINATIONS

The following vegetables lend themselves well to *bhaté* and *pora*

BHATÉ

Potol or Parwal
Kanchkola or raw green banana
Kochu or *Arvi*
Bandhakopi or cabbage
Korola or bitter gourd
Begun or Brinjal
Kumro or red pumpkin
Potatoes

PORA

Begun or brinjal
Aam or raw green mango
Potol or parwal
Capsicum or bell pepper

Bora

Fried Vegetable Balls

Bora is generally made from boiled vegetables or fresh ingredients like coconut. *Maacher dimer bora* (fried fish roe) is a real delicacy.

Bora can be served as a snack or along with a main meal.

Alu Bora

Fried Potato Balls

4 large potatoes
2 tablespoons besan
1 green chilli, chopped fine
2 tablespoons green coriander
　leaves, chopped
salt to taste
½ cup water
oil for frying

Scrub potatoes and then boil in water to cover, until soft. Drain water. Allow potatoes to cool and then peel. Mash well and add salt to taste, coriander leaves and green chilli. Mix well and add coriander leaves and green chilli. Mix well and form into small balls.

In a bowl whip the *besan* and water to a thin batter. Coat potato balls with this batter. Deep fry to a golden brown. Remove. Drain off oil. Serve hot.

A good accompaniment with: *Rice* and *dal* or *as a snack*

Serves: 4–6

Narkel Bora

Fried Coconut Balls

1 coconut, grated
a pinch turmeric powder
a pinch onion seeds
a pinch aniseed, roasted and
　powdered
2 green chillies, chopped fine
salt to taste
a tablespoon flour or rice flour
oil for frying

Grind the grated coconut to a dry paste on a curry stone. Mix all the other ingredients with the coconut and form into small balls.

Heat oil in pan, and deep fry coconut balls to a golden brown. Drain off oil. Serve hot.

A good accompaniment to: *Rice* and *dal* or *as a snack*

Serves: 4–6

Postor Bora

Fried Poppy-seed Balls

8 tablespoons poppy-seed
1 tablespoon flour or rice flour
2 green chillies, chopped very fine
1 onion, chopped fine
salt to taste
oil for frying.

Wash the poppy-seed well, then grind to a paste with very little water. Add all the other ingredients to the poppy-seed paste. Mix thoroughly.

Form into small balls and deep fry to a golden brown. Drain off oil and serve hot.

Serves: 4–6

Kumro Chenchki

Red Pumpkin fried with Spices

500 gms pumpkin, diced medium
   thick
2 tablespoons oil
1/8 teaspoon whole onion seeds
2 whole red chillies
1 onion, halved and sliced fine
1½ teaspoons turmeric paste
½ teaspoon chilli paste
salt to taste

Heat oil in a *karai*. When a blue haze appears, add the onion seeds and whole red chillies. Stir-fry for a couple of minutes and then add the pumpkin and some salt. Cover and cook for 2–3 minutes.

Remove cover. To the water given out by the pumpkin, add the sliced onion and *masala* pastes. Cook over high heat, stirring all the while. When the pumpkin is cooked and the oil rises to the surface, remove from fire.

This particular preparation of pumpkin is quite dry.

A good accompaniment with: *Rice, Luchi*

Serves: 6

Kumror Chhokka

Red Pumpkin with whole Chick-Peas

250 gms red pumpkin diced
2 tablespoons whole chola/chan-
    na soaked in water overnight
2 potatoes, peeled and diced
4 parwals, cut in quarter inch
    rounds (optional)
2 bay leaves
4 tablespoons oil
1/8 teaspoon panch phoran
a pinch of asafoetida
2–3 whole red chillies
1½ teaspoon turmeric paste
½ teaspoon chilli paste
1½ tablespoons cummin paste
½ tablespoon coriander paste
1 tablespoon ginger paste
1 tablespoon ghee
*1 teaspoon powdered garam
    masala
2 teaspoons sugar
salt to taste

*garam masala
2 green cardamon
2 cloves
2 inch piece cinnamon
2 bay leaves (small)

Heat oil in a *karai*. Add the bay leaves, *panch phoran*, asafoetida and whole red chillies. Stir-fry until spluttering stops. Add the *parwals* and fry 3 or 4 minutes before adding potatoes, continuing to fry a further 5 minutes. Then add the red pumpkin. Stir-fry until vegetables are all well fried. Now mix together in half or three-quarters cup water the *masala* pastes and pour over the vegetables. Add salt to taste.

Add the drained whole *chola* and simmer gently until vegetables are cooked and there is no gravy in the pan.

Heat *ghee* in a frying pan. Stir into the *chhokka* with the sugar.

Finally before removing from fire, sprinkle with the powdered *garam masala*.

A good accompaniment with: *Rice, Luchi* and *Porota*

Serves: 4

Moricher Jhol

A lightly spiced Vegetable Stew

2 cups stems and very young
  leaves of the marrow or
  pumpkin plant, cut in 1 inch
  or 1½ lengths. If pumpkin or
  marrow stems are unavailable,
  substitute with drumsticks
Vegetables as described under
  Shukto, cut in a similar manner (page 37)
8–10 green chillies, slit
6 kalai dal boris, fried crisp
1 tablespoon mustard oil
⅛ tps of turmeric paste
1 teaspoon ginger paste
2 teaspoons coriander paste
1 teaspoon ghee
⅛ tps of onion seeds
1 teaspoon cummin seeds*
2 green chillies*
½ teaspoon flour
2 tablespoons milk
salt and sugar to taste

*Coarsely ground together

Heat the mustard oil in a *karai*. Lightly fry the stems and leaves of the pumpkin or marrow together with the other vegetables. Add salt. Cover and cook for 5 minutes.

Add the turmeric, ginger and coriander pastes. Stir-fry several minutes, permitting the vegetables to cook in the water given out by them. Add the slit green chillies. Add a little additional water and simmer vegetables till done. Add the fried *bori*.

Remove from fire while there is still quite a lot of light gravy in pan. In a separate *karai* or pan, heat one teaspoon *ghee*. Add the onion seeds and stir-fry till the onion seeds stop spluttering. Pour into cooked vegetables and gravy in the *karai* and let it come to a boil. Simmer for 5 minutes.

Stir in the coarsely ground cummin seeds and green chillies. Simmer another 5 minutes.

Mix the flour and milk together and pour over vegetables. Adjust salt and add sugar to taste. Stir and simmer another 5 minutes. Remove from fire.

Variation:
This dish can also be cooked omitting turmeric, ginger and coriander.

A good accompaniment with: *Rice*

Serves: 6–8

Mochar Paturi and Thorer Chenchri

Murighonto

Potoler Dolma (Chanar Filling)

Pui Sager Chorhori

Jingé Posto

Ridge Gourd with Poppy-seeds

1 kg jhingé (ridge ground)
1 onion, finely sliced
2 tablespoons poppy seeds (posto),
   ground to a paste
1/4 teaspoon turmeric paste
1/4 teaspoon chilli paste
4 green chillies, chopped
3 tablespoons oil
1/4 teaspoon mustard seeds
2 whole red chillies
salt

Peel ridge gourd. Cut lengthwise in half and then horizontally into quarter inch semi-circles. Add salt and set aside in a colander for a while. Remove excess moisture by squeezing through fingers. Discard the water.

Heat oil in *karai* and fry the mustard seeds and red chillies for 2 minutes. Now add ridge gourd and fry for 5 minutes over brisk fire.

To the water that is given out by the ridge gourd, add the *masala* pastes, sliced onions and green chillies.

Add the poppy-seed paste, stir fry until the vegetable is quite dry and just turning brown.

A good accompaniment with: *Rice*

Serves: 6

Alu Posto

Potato with Poppy-seeds

This dish uses the same quantity of spices for 250 gms of potato with the addition of a cup of water.

Peel 250 gms medium sized potatoes and dice into cubes:

Heat oil in *karai*, fry mustard seeds and red chillies for 2 minutes. Sauté the diced potato in the *karai* till lightly brown, add *masala* paste, sliced onion, green chillies and a cup of water, cook for 5–7 minutes; add poppy seed paste, stir-fry on high heat till the potato is done and the poppy seed changes colour to a light golden brown.

Serves: 4

Kochu Sager Ghanto

A preparation with Colocassia Stems

The dark purple stems of the *Arvi* or Colocassia are used in this preparation and *not the leaves* as the name of the recipe indicates. In Bengal, we do not use the Arvi leaves for any preparations. The stems which are suitable for cooking are only available during the monsoons.

8 *young purple coloured arvi*
  stems
1 *tablespoon whole channa/chola*
  (soaked in water overnight)
½ *coconut, grated*
½ *tablespoon turmeric*
1 *teaspoon chilli paste*
1½ *tablespoons coriander paste*
2 *bay leaves*
⅛ *teaspoon whole cummin seeds*
2 *tablespoons oil*
1 *tablespoon ghee*
salt and sugar to taste

String or peel the *arvi* stems and cut in inch-pieces. Place in *dekchi* with water to cover and bring to boil. Throw away water and add fresh water. Repeat the procedure twice. Then boil until stems are soft. Drain well. Mash stems. Add all the *masala* pastes and mix well.

Heat oil in a *karai*. Add the whole *chola* and fry for a couple of minutes. Add the mashed stems and mix well. Add a quarter cup water, salt to taste and cook over medium hot fire, stirring all the time. When you can smell the *masalas* frying, add three-quarters of the grated coconut. Stir and mix well.

Heat *ghee* and fry the whole cummin seeds. Pour the *ghee* and cummin seeds over *Ghanto*. Stir and remove from fire. Garnish with the remaining coconut.

Variations:
1. Milk and sugar are sometimes added at the same time as the grated coconut.
2. *Kochu sag* is also cooked with the head of the hilsa. In this instance, the whole *chola*, coconut and milk are not included in the ingredients.

A good accompaniment with: *Rice*

Serves: 6–8

Lau Ghanto

A preparation with Bottle Gourd

500 gms *lau / lauki, finely diced*
6 *boris, fried or 1 tablespoon*
  parboiled mung dal, fried
2 *tablespoons oil*
2 *whole red chillies*
a *pinch whole cummin seeds*
½ *tablespoon turmeric paste*
1 *tablespoon coriander paste*
½ *teaspoon chilli paste*
3–4 *green chillies, slit*
1 *teaspoon ghee*
salt and sugar to taste
1 *tablespoon coriander leaves*
  (optional), chopped

Heat oil in *karai*, add the red chillies and whole cummin seeds. When spluttering stops, add the *lau* and salt. Stir, cover and cook for 5 minutes. Now add to the *lau* all the *masala* pastes and sugar to taste. Stir and cook over high heat until nearly all the water is absorbed. Add the parboiled *mung dal* or *bori* and the green chillies. Stir-cook until all the water is all absorbed and vegetable is cooked. It may be necessary to add a little water at the time of adding the *mung dal* or *bori*.

Heat *ghee* and add to the vegetable. Stir in the chopped coriander leaves, adjust seasoning and remove from fire.

A good accompaniment with: *Rice* or *Luchi*

Serves: 4

Kopir Muri Ghanto

Spiced Cauliflower with Rice

1 cauliflower (approx 350–400
    gms), cut in small flowerets
2 tablespoons rice, washed and
    drained
1 teaspoon turmeric paste
½ teaspoon chilli paste
1 tablespoon cummin paste
½ tablespoon coriander paste
½ teaspoon garam masala paste
garam masala (see page 7)
2 bay leaves
8 tablespoons oil
1 tablespoon ghee
1 cup water
salt and sugar to taste

Heat oil and fry the cauliflower until just brown.
Remove from pan.

Add all the *masalas* to the pan (except bay leaves
and *garam masala* paste) and fry for several minutes,
sprinkling water if necessary.

When the *masalas* are done, add the rice; fry again
for several minutes, sprinkling water if necessary.

When the rice is well fried (about 5–7 minutes),
add a cup of water, salt and sugar to taste. Cover
pan and simmer over medium heat until rice is nearly
done, but not dry.

Add the cauliflower. Mix well, cover and cook for
several minutes longer.

By this time, rice and cauliflower should be well
cooked and there should still be some gravy in the
pan.

Stir in the *garam masala* paste.

In a separate pan, heat *ghee* and fry the bay leaves
and *garam masala* for a couple of minutes. Pour over
cauliflower-rice mixture.

Stir and remove the *Kopir Muri Ghanto* from fire.

A good accompaniment with: *Rice* or *Luchi*

Serves: 5

Mulor Ghanto

Curried Horse Radish

4 horse radish or large white
   mooli, diced
2 large potatoes, diced
100 gms green peas, shelled
½ tablespoon turmeric paste
1 teaspoon chilli paste
1½ tablespoons aniseed paste
2 tablespoons oil
1 teaspoon ghee
1 teaspoon garam masala paste
   (see page 7)
2 whole red chillies
a pinch of whole cummin seeds
salt to taste
sugar to taste

Parboil the horse radish. Drain and squeeze out the water.

Lightly brown the diced potatoes and keep aside.

Add the whole red chillies and cummin seeds to the hot oil in a *karai* and stir-fry a couple of minutes. Add the horse radish, stir and add all the *masala* pastes, salt and sugar to taste. Cover and cook for 5 minutes. Add the potatoes and peas. Stir and simmer until all the vegetables are done. Add a little water, if necessary, while cooking.

Before removing from fire, heat a teaspoon *ghee* and fry *garam masala* paste. Stir into vegetable.

Variation:
100 gms shrimps may be added with the peas or instead of peas.

This dish can be made with *olkopi* (*ganth gobi* or knol khol), using the same quantities as for horse radish.

A good accompaniment with: *Rice, Luchi* or *Porota*

Serves: 4

Palong Sager Ghanto

A preparation of Spinach with other vegetables

½ kg spinach
1 large brinjal
1 large horse radish
2 potatoes
¼ of a medium cauliflower
½ cup peas, shelled
4–6 medium sized bori, fried and
   crumbled (optional)
½ grated coconut
4–6 green chillies
1 tablespoon turmeric paste
½ tablespoon chilli paste
2 tablespoons ground cummin
   paste
1½ tablespoons coriander paste
¼ teaspoon panch phoran
salt and sugar to taste
about ½ cup oil

Trim the spinach, removing hard stalks, wash well, drain off water. Put spinach in a medium sized *dekchi*, add a little salt, cover and let it cook in its own juice. Sprinkle a little water if necessary. Remove from fire when quite limp and cooked. Mash fine.

In the meantime, dice the brinjal, radish and potatoes and cut the cauliflower into very small flowerettes.

Heat oil in a pan, fry the vegetables one at a time till lightly browned and keep aside.

Using the same pan heat approximately 2 tablespoons oil (oil in which vegetables were fried may be used). Add *panch phoran* and when spluttering stops, add the spinach and then add all the *masalas*. Mix well and cook for about 10 minutes or until the *masala* and the spinach appear cooked. Add a sprinkle of water if spinach begins to stick to pan.

Then add the vegetables and green chillies. Continue cooking another 10 minutes or so, adding quarter cup water if pan is quite dry. Add additional salt and 1 tablespoon   sugar, if preferred. Then add half the grated coconut, mix well and remove the pan from fire.

Pour *ghanto* into serving dish. Sprinkle with balance coconut and crumbled fried *bori*.

A good accompaniment with: *Rice*

Serves: 4–6

Chorchori and Chanchra

I have given some conventional and popular recipes for *chorchori* but anything and everything edible can go into the making of a *chorchori;* vegetable stems or the stems of other greens which would normally be thrown away can be cut and used. Apart from these vegetables others can be added including the peel of several. The only vegetables which must be included are horse radish, red pumpkin, brinjals, potatoes and some form of *sag*.

In the *chanchra* the discarded portions of a large fish, such as the head and bones, are cut and included with the vegetables after first being lightly fried in a little oil. Quite often, the edible innards of the fish, washed well and cut are included. The head and entrails of the hilsa are often used in *chanchra* and sometimes shrimps or prawn heads replace the fish. Apart from this, there is little difference in the preparation of *chorchori* and *chanchra* and the spices used are the same.

Alu Piajer Chorchori
Dry Curried Potato and Onion

*5 medium sized potatoes, cut in
  half lengthwise and then sliced
  in 1/8 inch pieces crosswise
4 onions, cut in half lengthwise,
  and then sliced thickly than
  normal
2 teaspoons turmeric paste
1/2 teaspoon chilli paste
4–6 green chillies, washed and slit
salt to taste
2 tablespoons oil
1/2 cup water or as required*

Heat oil when blue haze appears, add potatoes and fry for several minutes until potatoes turn opaque. Reduce heat, add onions and continue to fry, stirring now and then for another couple of minutes.

Add the turmeric, chilli paste and salt to taste, mixing thoroughly and continue to fry. Add green chillies.

The potatoes and onions should cook as much as possible in their own juices, but if it gets too dry, test to see how much cooking the potatoes require and accordingly add water a little at a time.

The cooked dish is dry and, therefore, adding of water should be judicious. The dish is cooked when the potatoes are done and there is practically no gravy.

Can be reheated before serving.

A good accompaniment with: *Rice, Luchi* or *Porota*

Serves: 4–6

Bati Chorchori
Dry Mixed Vegetables

200 gms cauliflower, cut into
   small flowerettes
100 gms green peas, shelled
2 potatoes, peeled and cubed
1 medium brinjal, cubed
1 horse radish or mooli, peeled
   and cubed
1/4 onion, minced
1 teaspoon turmeric paste
1/2 teaspoon chilli paste
2 teaspoons mustard paste
3–4 green chillies, slit
4–6 tablespoons mustard oil
salt to taste

This particular preparation should be cooked in a recepticle in which the ingredients fit snugly, leaving a gap of one inch or so at the top. Conventionally, a brass bowl or *bati* is used. This may be substituted by an aluminium *bati* or *dekchi* with a tight fitting lid.

After cutting all the vegetables, wash well and place in a *bati* or *dekchi*. Add the minced onion, the *masala* pastes and green chillies. Add the oil and mix well after adding salt. Cover with tight fitting lid.

Place over very gentle fire and cook, stirring from time to time. The vegetables will cook in their own juices without addition of any water. Remove from fire when vegetables are quite cooked and blended with the *masalas*.

Variation:
100 gms shelled shrimps may be added. *Bati Chorchori* is also made with various other small fish.

Any suitable combination of vegetables may be used in preparing *Bati Chorchori*.

Microwave
Mix ingredients in a glass bowl with a tight fitting lid or cover dish with cling flim. Cook on high for 10 mins, open lid/cling film. Stir the ingredients well. Replace lid/cling film and cook further for 15 minutes on medium. Let it stand for 5 minutes, before removing lid, serve

A good accompaniment with: *Rice*

Serves: 4–6

Dharosh or Bhindi Chorchori

Ladies' Fingers or Okra with Masala

250 gms ladies' fingers
1 onion, halved and sliced
salt to taste
1½ teaspoons turmeric paste
½ teaspoon chilli paste
2–3 green chillies
2 tablespoons oil
⅛ panch phoran

Slice off the stem and tip of the ladies' fingers. With a knife make a couple of gashes on the body of the vegetable.

Heat oil in a *karai* or pan. Add *panch phoran* and cook until spluttering stops. Add the ladies' fingers. Stir-fry about 5 minutes, add salt. Add the *masala* paste and the sliced onion. Stir and cook a couple of minutes, then add half cup water. Add the green chillies.

Simmer over medium heat until ladies' fingers are cooked, the pan nearly dry and oil has come to the surface.

A good accompaniment with: *Rice*

Serves: 4

Khosha Chorchori

Dry fried Vegetable Peels

2 cups peel from bottle gourd,
    pumpkin and potatoes, washed
    thoroughly and julienned
2 onions halved and sliced very
    fine
1 teaspoon turmeric paste
½ teaspoon chilli paste
3–4 green chillies, split
2 tablespoons oil
¼ teaspoon panch phoran

Heat oil in pan. Add *panch phoran*. Cook until it stops spluttering.

Add the *masalas* and fry 3–4 minutes, then add the julienned peel and the onions.

Continue frying until onions become soft and the peel is cooked. If too dry while cooking, sprinkle water as and when necessary.

A good accompaniment with: *Rice*

Serves: 3–4

Pui Sager Chorchori

6 cups pui sag, chopped
4 medium potatoes, unpeeled,
    halved lengthwise and then cut
    crosswise—1/4 inch thick
2 brinjals (medium) or 1 large,
    quartered lengthwise and cut
    into 1 inch pieces
1 large horse radish-mooli cut in
    half lengthwise, peeled and
    then cut into 1 inch pieces
1 sweet potato, if available, cut to
    a similar size
12 pieces red pumpkin, the same
    size as horse radish, unpeeled
    (approx 250 gms)
1 onion, halved and sliced
1/4 teaspoon panch phoran
1 teaspoon turmeric paste
1 tablespoon mustard paste
1 tablespoon cummin paste
1/2 tablespoon coriander paste
1/2 tablespoon chilli paste
1 tablespoon sugar (optional)
2 tablespoons mustard oil
salt to taste

Heat oil in *karai*. Add *panch phoran* and fry till the spices stop spluttering. Add the *pui sag* and salt and mix well. Cover *karai* with a suitable lid and allow to simmer for 5 minutes. Remove lid. The *sag* would have wilted to nearly half its original quantity.

Now add all the vegetables to the *sag* and mix thoroughly.

Next stir in all *masalas*, the chopped onion and sugar if preferred.

Cover and allow to simmer for another 5 minutes. Remove lid and continue cooking, stirring from time to time, until nearly all the water is absorbed.

The vegetable in the *chorchori* should cook in the water from the *pui sag*. If the quantity of water is excessive, the *chorchori* must be cooked over high heat so that the vegetables do not disintegrate completely. When ready the *chorchori* should be nearly dry.

Variation:
Palang Chorchori—Spinach with Vegetables

1 kg spinach can replace *pui sag* in making *chorchori*. The same ingredients are used. The only difference is in the method of cooking.

Fry the vegetables first, next stir in all the *masalas*, the chopped onions and sugar if preferred. Add a little water if vegetables get too dry. The spinach should be added about 10 minutes before end of cooking time and mixed in well.

Best with *rice*

Serves: 8–10

Sajne Dantar Chorchori

Drumsticks with Vegetables

4–6 drumsticks, string and cut in
    3 inch lengths
2 potatoes, scrubbed, halved and
    sliced a quarter-inch thick un-
    peeled
12 one-inch pieces red pumpkin.
    with skin approx 250 gms
2 medium sized brinjals, halved
    and cut in one-inch pieces with
    skin
1 horse radish, peeled and cut in
    1-inch lengths (optional)
4 parwals, scraped, split
    lengthwise and halved again
    (optional)
1 onion, halved and sliced fine
1/2 tablespoon turmeric paste
1/2 teaspoon coriander paste
    (optional)
1 teaspoon chilli paste
1 teaspoon cummin paste
    (optional)
1 teaspoon mustard paste
a pinch panch phoran
2 tablespoons mustard oil

Heat oil in *karai*. Add *panch phoran*. When splutter-ing stops add potatoes, horse radish, *parwal*. Stir-fry 5 minutes. Add drumsticks and salt. Cover and cook 5 minutes.

Add all the *masala* pastes. Stir.

Add the remaining vegetables. Stir and cover, cook another 5–7 minutes.

Add half cup water and simmer until all vegetables are cooked and well blended with the *masalas*. There should be practically no gravy in the pan.

Serves: 4–6

Sheem Begun Chorchori

Flat Beans and Brinjal

100–125 gms sheem
2 medium sized potatoes
2 medium sized brinjals
1 large onion, finely sliced
1½ tablespoons oil
⅛ teaspoon panch phoran
1½ teaspoons turmeric paste
¼ teaspoon chilli paste
salt to taste
3–4 green chillies, slit (optional)

String and cut the *sheem* in half. Halve the brinjals and cut into three-quarter inch thick pieces. Scrub the potatoes. Cut in half lengthwise without peeling and then slice crosswise, into quarter-inch thick pieces.

Heat oil in *karai*. Add *panch phoran* to the hot oil and stir-fry until spluttering stops.

Add all the vegetables and some salt. Stir, cover pan and simmer 5–7 minutes. Remove cover and stir in the sliced onions and *masala* pastes. Cover again and simmer gently another 5–7 minutes. Remove cover and stir. If there is no water given off from the vegetables, add a quarter to half cup water.

Cook over medium heat stirring from time to time until all vegetables are cooked, the *masalas* have blended in well with the vegetables, there is practically no gravy left in the pan and oil has come to the surface.

Note: The nearest substitute for *sheem* is flat beans or mange-tout.

A good accompaniment with: *Rice*

Serves: 4

Begun Sorsé

Brinjals with Mustard

500 gms brinjals
1 tablespoon turmeric paste
1 teaspoon chilli paste
100 gms dahi
1/2 cup water
1 1/2 tablespoons mustard paste,
    finely ground
1/8 teaspoon panch phoran
4–5 green chillies
oil for frying
salt and sugar to taste

Cut the brinjals in large pieces. Rub with a little turmeric and salt. Heat oil in a fry pan and fry brinjals until brown and nearly cooked. Remove and drain off oil.

Take 2 tablespoons of the oil in which brinjals were cooked and heat in a *karai* or pan till smoking. Add *panch phoran* and green chillies. Fry till spluttering stops. Add turmeric and chilli pastes. Sprinkle a little water and fry the *masalas* well. Whip the *dahi* and add to the fried *masalas*. Stir and cook a couple of minutes. Add the brinjals. Stir and continue simmering another 5–10 minutes. Add the finely ground mustard paste. Mix well.

Continue simmering until mustard paste has blended in, and there is very little gravy in the pan.

Note: Freshly prepared English mustard may be substituted for the ground mustard paste.

A good accompaniment with: *Rice*

Serves: 4–6

Dharosh or Bhindi Sorsé

Ladies' Fingers or Okra cooked with Mustard

250 gms ladies' fingers
2 tablespoons oil
1/8 teaspoon onion seeds
2 tablespoons mustard paste*
1/2 teaspoon turmeric paste*
1/2 teaspoon chilli paste*
3–4 green chillies slit
salt to taste

*blended together in
1/2 cup water

Slice off the stem and tip of the ladies' fingers; otherwise leave whole. Make a couple of gashes on the body of the vegetable.

Heat oil in a *karai*. Add the onion seeds and fry till they stop spluttering. Add the ladies' fingers and stir-fry for at least 5 minutes, adding salt to taste. When the vegetables appear fried but not brown, add the *masala* paste blended with water. Stir and add the green chillies.

Simmer gently until the ladies' fingers are cooked and there is only a thick gravy in the pan.

If necessary, a little additional water may be added, depending on how long the vegetables take to cook.

A good accompaniment with: *Rice*

Serves: 4–6

Jhingé Kumro Paturi

Red Pumpkin and Ridge Gourd cooked on Banana Leaves

500 gms jinghé (tori)
250 gms red pumpkin
2 onions, very finely sliced
1 teaspoon turmeric paste
1/4 teaspoon chilli paste
2 1/2 tablespoons mustard paste
4 green chillies, chopped fine
1/2 coconut, grated
salt to taste
1/4 cup or 60 gms mustard oil
6 banana leaves, cut to size for iron tawa

Peel the *jhingé* and cut fine. Add half a teaspoon salt and leave for a while. With the addition of salt, the *jhingé* will give out water. Squeeze this out and keep aside.

Peel and cut the pumpkin into julienne strips. In a bowl mix together the two vegetables and all the other ingredients. Be cautious when adding salt because both the *jhingé* and pumpkin reduce considerably when cooked.

Place the banana leaves crosswise on the tawa and place on the fire over medium heat. Pour the vegetable mixture onto the banana leaves and cook, increasing heat towards end of cooking time until vegetables are cooked and oil comes to the surface.

Turn vegetables over once during cooking and smooth over with the back of a spoon.

Microwave method
Mix all ingredients together, place on a piece of washed banana leaf and cover with another piece to make a packet. Place this in a glass dish, cover with cling film/lid and cook on high for 10 mins. Turn the packet, cover with cling film/lid, reduce power to medium and cook for another 10 mins—let it stand for 5 mins before opening packet. Serve from the banana leaf.

Note: Courgettes or zucchini can be substituted for *jhingé*.

A good accompaniment with: *Rice*

Serves: 6

Monama

Cauliflower with Mustard

Monama was a distant relative of my mother. A widow, she lived in what was in the early thirties, the village of Dum Dum, now almost swallowed up by the International Airport complex for Calcutta. One of our greatest pleasures as young children was to go with our mother to spend the day with Monama.

Monama was a fabulous cook. I can still remember, young as I was then, the day she first cooked cauliflower with mustard for us. We all liked it so much that my mother asked her for the recipe. It has become a family favourite and is known in our family as just 'Monama'.

1 young cauliflower, approx
  1 kg, cut in small flowerettes
1 teaspoon turmeric paste
4–6 tablespoons mustard, ground
  (preferably a mixture of the
  black and white varieties and
  the exact amount depends on
  preference)
1 cup water
8 tablespoons mustard oil
salt to taste
6–10 green chillies, washed
  and slit

Heat oil in pan and when blue haze appears, add cauliflowerettes and fry until very lightly browned.

In 1 cup water; mix 1 teaspoon turmeric paste and ground mustard paste. Pour into pan through a fine sieve.

Add green chillies and salt.

Reduce heat, cook over medium flame until practically dry.

Remove from heat.

Variation:
Add ½ teaspoon of onion seeds to heated oil prior to frying cauliflower.

A good accompaniment with: *Rice*

Serves: 4

Sajné Sorsé

Drumsticks cooked with Mustard

12 drumsticks
1 onion, halved and sliced
   very fine
2 tablespoons mustard paste
1/8 teaspoon turmeric paste or
   powder
1/8 teaspoon chilli paste
1 cup water
4–6 green chillies, slit
a pinch onion seeds
1 tablespoon mustard oil
salt to taste

String drumsticks and cut into 3–4 inch lengths.

Blend together the *masala* pastes with 1 cup water. Heat oil in *karai* and fry the onion seeds till spluttering stops. Add the drumsticks and sliced onion. Stir and fry till onions turn opaque.

Add the *masala* water through a sieve. Add salt to taste and the slit green chillies. Stir and simmer until nearly dry and oil has come to the surface.

A good accompaniment with: Rice

Serves: 4

Sheem Sorsé

Flat Beans cooked with Mustard

250 gms fresh young sheem
1 onion, halved and sliced fine
2 tablespoons mustard paste
1/2 teaspoon turmeric paste
1/4 teaspoon chilli paste
3–4 green chillies, slit
2 tablespoons oil, preferably
   mustard oil
1/2 cup water
salt to taste

String *sheem* and slice on the bias like french beans, approx. half inch thick. In half cup of water, mix together all the *masala* pastes and keep aside. Heat oil in *karai* or pan, add sliced onion and when well fried but not brown, add the sliced *sheem*.

Stir-fry a few minutes, but before the vegetable turns brown, add the half cup water into which the *masala* pastes have been blended. Add salt to taste and the green chillies.

Bring to boil and then gently simmer until practically all the water is absorbed and oil rises to the surface.

A good accompaniment with: *Rice*

Serves: 4

Bandhakopir Misti Dalna

Cabbage cooked with Coconut and Milk

500 gms cabbage, sliced fine
1/2 fresh coconut, grated
6–8 green chillies, slit
1 tablespoon oil
1/8 teaspoon mustard seeds
1/4 cup milk
1/2 teaspoon flour
salt to taste
1 to 1 1/2 teaspoons sugar

Heat oil in a *karai*. Add the mustard seeds and when this stops spluttering add the cabbage.

Add salt to the cabbage. Stir and cover. Simmer 5–7 minutes. Remove cover and cook over medium flame until nearly cooked. If necessary, add a little water.

When cabbage is nearly done and practically dry, add all but 2 tablespoons of grated coconut. Also add the green chillies. Stir and continue cooking until cabbage is done.

Mix together the milk and flour. Stir into cabbage along with the sugar. Stir-fry until milk is absorbed into the cabbage.

Remove from fire and sprinkle with the remaining 2 tablespoons of the grated coconut.

A good accompaniment with: *Rice*

Serves: 4–6

Lauer Misti Dalna

Delicately Spiced Vegetable Marrow with Sugar

4 cups diced lau or bottle gourd
6–8 green chillies, split
    nearly in half
2 tablespoons coriander leaves
1/4 teaspoon turmeric (optional)
1/4 cup milk
sugar and salt to taste
1/4 teaspoon onion seeds
1 tablespoon oil

Heat oil and add onion seeds and cook a couple of minutes or until they stop spluttering. Add *lau* and salt to taste. Mix well and cover pan and cook for 5–7 minutes. Remove lid from pan and add turmeric, mixing well again. Cook *lau* in its own juice, stirring from time to time to ensure that it does not stick to the bottom of the pan. Add the green chillies. When nearly all the water in the pan is absorbed, add the quarter cup milk and sugar as preferred. Finally add chopped coriander leaves. Mix well.

The *dalna* is ready when the milk is absorbed and the *lau* cooked.

Variation :
Freshly grated coconut may be added to the *dalna* 5 minutes before it is finally removed from the fire. Before serving fried *bori* crumbled may also be added.

A good accompaniment with: *Rice*

Serves: 4

Misti Dalna

Delicately Spiced Mixed Vegetables with Sugar

3 potatoes, peeled and quartered
6 parwals, scraped and halved
12 one-inch piece pumpkin peeled
   (approx 250 gms)
12 pieces medium cauliflowerettes
   (approx 250 gms)
salt to taste
6–8 green chillies, slit
½ cup water, ¼ cup milk
1 to 2 teaspoons sugar
oil for frying vegetables
2 tablespoons ghee
garam masala, whole (see page 7)
2 bay leaves

Heat oil in pan and fry each vegetable separately until just turning brown. Drain oil from pan, sieve and keep aside for other uses. In the same pan heat 2 tablespoons *ghee*. Add bay leaves and *garam masala* and fry a couple of minutes. Add the fried vegetables and mix thoroughly with the *garam masala*. Add first half cup water and the green chillies. Simmer over low heat until nearly dry. Add the milk, salt and sugar to taste. Continue cooking till just a very little liquid remains in the pan and the vegetables are cooked.

A good accompaniment with: *Rice*

Serves: 4

Alur Dom—Basic

Potato Curry

1 kg small potatoes, unpeeled
100 gms onion, chopped
150 gms onion paste
3 teaspoons turmeric paste
1 teaspoon red chilli paste
2 tablespoons ghee
1 teaspoon salt
1 teaspoon sugar
2 cups water
garam masala (see page 7)
2 bay leaves

Boil the potatoes in water, till just done. Drain in colander and pour cold water over them. Cool and then peel.

Heat *ghee* till very hot. Fry chopped onions till golden brown. Add onion paste and cook a couple of minutes, then add turmeric and red chilli paste. Cook without adding any water, but without burning the *masalas,* for about 5 minutes. Add 2 cups water and let it come to the boil. Add boiled potatoes, sugar and salt and simmer until liquid is reduced to half. In a separate pan heat 1 teaspoon *ghee.* Add *garam masala* and bay leaves. Fry for a couple of minutes and pour onto the potatoes. Stir and cook a couple of minutes longer and then remove from heat.

Variation :
Add 2 or 3 medium sized tomatoes chopped at the same time as other *masalas* are added and then continue cooking as above.

Add 250 gms *dahi* after *masalas* are fried. Reduce heat after adding *dahi* and simmer for 5 minutes. Then add water and continue as above.

A good accompaniment with: *Rice, Luchi, Porota*

Serves: 6–8

Alur Dom (2)

Potato Curry

1 kg small potatoes
1 tablespoon coriander paste
3 tablespoons cummin paste
1½ tablespoons black pepper
    paste (or less if preferred)
¼ teaspoon turmeric paste
garam masala (see page 7)
2 bay leaves
1–1½ cups water
1–1½ teaspoons salt
1–1½ teaspoons sugar
125 gms or ½ cup ghee

Boil and cool potatoes as described earlier. Peel.

In a saucepan, heat *ghee* to a high heat, add bay leaves and *garam masala*. Fry for 2 minutes and then add all the *masalas*. Cook *masalas* over high heat for 5 minutes, then add water. Let the gravy come to a boil. Add potatoes. Allow it to boil again for about 5 minutes. Reduce heat to medium, add salt, sugar and cook until all the water is absorbed.

This is a dry *alur dom* and very popular as a cocktail snack.

Variation:
Add 2–3 medium tomatoes chopped to the *masalas* and then continue cooking as above.

Add 2 tablespoons of thick tamarind juice during final stage of cooking.

A good accompaniment with: *Radhaballobhi, Luchi, Porota*

Serves: 6–8

Alu-Potoler Dalna

Curried Potatoes and Parwal

8–12 parwals, scrubbed and
    halved
4 potatoes, peeled and quartered
1½ tablespoons coriander paste
1 tablespoon cummin paste
1 teaspoon chilli paste
2 bay leaves
½ teaspoon whole cummin seeds
salt and sugar to taste
4 tablespoons oil
1 tablespoon ghee

Heat oil in *karai* and fry the potatoes and *parwals* separately until lightly browned. Remove from pan and keep aside.

In oil, in the same pan, add all the *masala* pastes, salt and sugar to taste. Stir fry the *masalas* until colour changes, sprinkling water as necessary. When *masalas* are cooked, add 1¼ to 2 cups water. Bring to the boil and then simmer gently for 5 minutes. Add the potatoes and *parwals*. Cook stirring from time to time until very little gravy remains in pan and the vegetables are cooked.

In a separate frying pan or *karai*, heat the *ghee* and stir-fry the bay leaves and whole cummin seeds until spluttering stops. Pour onto *Alu-Potoler Dalna*. Stir and remove from fire.

Variations:
Brown a chopped onion in the oil before adding *masalas*. Also include one onion ground to the *masala* pastes. In this instance, however, I reduce the quantity of coriander and cummin paste to one teaspoon each. Substitute whole *garam masala* instead of whole cummin seeds.

A good accompaniment with: *Rice, Luchi, Ghee Bhat*

Serves: 4–6

Alu-Phulkopir Dalna

Potato and Cauliflower Curry

½ kg potatoes, cut in quarters
1 kg cauliflower, cut in medium-
sized flowerettes
4 medium tomatoes, cut in
quarters
150 gms onion, chopped fine
1 tablespoon turmeric paste
1 teaspoon chilli paste
2 tablespoons coriander paste
1 tablespoon cummin paste
4 tablespoons mustard oil
2 tablespoons ghee
1 to 1½ cups water
garam masala (see page 7)
2 bay leaves

Heat mustard oil in pan and when very hot fry the potatoes lightly (about 10 minutes) and remove. Then fry the cauliflowerettes till just turning brown. Remove pan from fire. Drain oil from cauliflowerettes (oil can be filtered clear and re-used).

In the same pan, add *ghee*. Bring to high heat, add bay leaves and *garam masala*. Fry 2–3 minutes. Add chopped onions, fry to a golden brown (about 15 minutes).

Add *masalas* and fry 5 minutes, taking care it does not stick to the bottom of the pan. If necessary, add a tablespoon of water while frying. Add fried potatoes, cauliflowerettes and tomatoes and mix thoroughly with *masalas*.

Add water, cover and cook over medium heat. Remove cover and stir from time to time. Remove from heat when nearly dry.

Alu-Phulkopir Dalna may be cooked ahead and re-heated just before serving. Care should be taken to see that the potatoes and cauliflowerettes do not disintegrate while being cooked. Colour should be a light golden yellow.

A good accompaniment with: *Rice, Luchi, Porota, Ghee Bhat*

Serves: 8–10

Bandhakopir Dalna

Dry Cabbage Curry

500 gms cabbage, sliced fine
2 potatoes, cut in small cubes
1½ tablespoons oil
1 tablespoon turmeric paste
1¼ to 2 teaspoons chilli paste
1¼ tablespoon cummin paste
1 tablespoon coriander paste
1 teaspoon ginger paste (optional)
1 tablespoon ghee
2 bay leaves
garam masala (see page 7)
salt and sugar to taste

Fry the cubed potatoes in hot oil in a *karai* until lightly browned. Remove from oil and keep aside. To the hot oil in *karai*, add the cabbage. Sprinkle with salt. Stir and cover *karai*. Simmer covered for 5 minutes. Remove cover. To the water given out by the cabbage, add the *masala* pastes. Stir and fry until *masalas* are well blended with the cabbage. If the cabbage is young, it should be nearly cooked at this stage.

Add ¼ to ½ cup water—just sufficient to cook the potatoes. Stir and add potatoes. Adjust salt and add sugar to taste. Simmer over medium heat until potatoes are cooked and there is practically no gravy in the pan.

In a frying pan, heat the tablespoon *ghee*. Add the bay leaves and *garam masala*. Stir-fry a couple of minutes and pour over *Bandhakopir Dalna*. Stir the cabbage and remove from fire.

Variations:
Add a couple of diced tomatoes to the cabbage along with the *masala* pastes.

Add 100 gms fried shelled shrimps to the cabbage at the same time as the potatoes or 100 gms fresh peas.

Add a tablespoon chopped coriander leaves just before removing from fire.

Instead of *garam masala*, whole cummin seeds may be substituted for a change.

A good accompaniment with: *Rice, Luchi, Porota* or *Ghee Bhat*

Serves: 4–6

Chhanar Dalna

Fresh Cottage Cheese Curry

250 gms chhana
3 potatoes, quartered lengthwise
   and then cut in half across to
   make 24 pieces
100 gms peas
½ tablespoon turmeric paste
1 teaspoon chilli paste
½ teaspoon cummin paste
1½ teaspoons coriander paste
salt and sugar to taste
2 tablespoons oil
1 tablespoon ghee
a pinch of whole cummin seeds

Shape *chhana* in an oblong, half inch thick piece and keep under weight until ready to use. Cut into 1 inch squares and fry till lightly browned. Keep aside.

Fry the potatoes till lightly browned in the same oil. Keep aside.

To the oil remaining in the *karai*, add 1 tablespoon *ghee* and when hot, put in the whole cummin seeds. When spluttering stops, add all the *masala* pastes. Stir-fry for several minutes. Add the green peas and continue to fry sprinkling with water. Add salt and sugar to taste. When *masalas* are well fried, add 1½ cups water. Bring to boil. Add the fried potatoes, cover *karai* and simmer until potatoes are half cooked. Add the *chhana* cubes. Stir and cook until potatoes are done and oil has risen to the surface. There should be some gravy in the pan.

A good accompaniment with: *Rice, Luchi, Ghee Bhat*

Serves: 4

Enchorer Dalna

Curried Green Jackfruit

500 gms enchor or green jackfruit
4 potatoes
2 tablespoons coriander paste
1 tablespoon cummin paste
1½ teaspoons turmeric paste
1 teaspoon chilli paste
1 teaspoon garam masala paste
* or powder (see page 7)*
2–3 bay leaves
¼ teaspoon whole cummin seeds
3 tablespoons oil
1 tablespoon ghee
salt and sugar to taste

Peel off the outer skin of the jackfruit. Remove seeds, if any. Also throw away the fibrous portion of the jackfruit retaining only the 'meaty' portion. There is a layer of skin between the seed and the fruit. Ensure that this is also removed and thrown away.

Cut the jackfruit in bite size or a little larger pieces. Place in a pan with water to cover and boil for approximately 15 minutes. Remove from fire. Drain well. Peel and cut the potatoes in four lengthwise and then cut across to make 8 pieces. Heat oil in *karai*. Fry the potatoes until lightly browned. Remove from pan. Add all the *masala* pastes, salt and sugar to taste to the pan. Stir well and fry several minutes sprinkling water as necessary. Continue stirring and frying until *masalas* change colour.

Add one cup water, stir and add the boiled *enchor* and the potatoes. Simmer gently until the potatoes and *enchor* are both cooked and there is a small amount of gravy in the pan.

In a separate pan or *karai*, heat 1 tablespoon of *ghee*. Add the bay leaves and whole cummin seeds. Stir-fry until the *masalas* stop spluttering. Pour on to *Enchor Dalna*. Stir well.

Variation:
A half cup peeled and shelled shrimps previously sautéed in a little oil may be added to the *Enchor Dalna* when it is simmering after addition of water.

Two chopped tomatoes may be added to the *masalas* and fried along with them.

A good accompaniment with: *Rice*

Serves: 6–8

Kumro Bothi

Pumpkin with Coconut

1 kg red pumpkin
½ fresh coconut, grated
1 teaspoon turmeric paste
½ teaspoon chilli paste
2 tablespoons cummin paste
1 tablespoon coriander paste
green chillies
2 tablespoons oil
¼ teaspoon panch phoran
2 bay leaves
3–4 dry red chillies
1 tablespoon ghee or oil
salt to taste

Slice the red pumpkin into very thin 1-inch sticks after removing skin and the inner portion with seeds.

Heat the oil in a *karai* and then add the sliced pumpkin. Add salt, mix well, cover and leave for about 5–7 minutes. Be careful of the quantity of salt added because pumpkin reduces considerably when cooked. Remove cover from pan. Add all the *masalas*. Mix well. Continue cooking over a reasonably brisk fire, stirring from time to time. Add the green chillies and continue to cook until nearly all the water given out from the pumpkin disappears. Stir in about two-thirds of the grated coconut, mixing well. Continue cooking stirring all the time for another 5–7 minutes. Remove from fire. In a separate pan heat 1 tablespoon oil. Add *panch phoran,* bay leaves and red chillies. When the *panch phoran* stops spluttering, add the cooked pumpkin. Mix thoroughly. Cook for 2 minutes. Remove from fire. Sprinkle over with the remaining coconut.

Microwave method
Mix together pumpkin, salt, sugar, oil and *masala* pastes. Place in a suitable dish with a tight fitting lid on cover with cling film—cook on high power for 10 mins. Remove lid and stir in green chillies, cook on medium power for another 8 mins, add grated coconut, mix well cook on high for another 2–3 mins. Let it stand for 5 mins. Follow as above.

A good accompaniment with: *Rice, Luchi*

Serves: 6

Pépér Dalna

Green Papaya Curry

*½ kg green papaya, peeled and
  cut in small thin slices*
1½ tablespoons coriander paste
¼ teaspoon turmeric paste
½ tablespoon cummin paste
*2 green chillies, chopped in
  4-6 pieces*
2 bay leaves
¼ teaspoon whole onion seeds
salt and sugar to taste
2 tablespoons ghee

First boil the green papaya in water to cover for about 10 minutes. Drain off all the water.

In a *karai* or pan, heat 1½ tablespoons *ghee*. Add the bay leaves and onion seeds and cook till spluttering stops. Now add the boiled green papaya, stir and add all the *masala* pastes and salt and sugar to taste. Cover and cook for about 5 minutes. Remove cover, add green chillies and continue cooking, stirring from time to time until all the water from the papaya has dried up. If papaya is not quite cooked, add a little water.

Heat half tablespoon *ghee* separately and pour over *dalna*. Stir and remove from fire.

Optional: Fried *bori* can be added to the papaya at the same time as the green chillies, if this is preferred.

Green peas can be added about the same time as green chillies or a handful of soaked *channa* (whole chick-peas) can be added along with green chillies.

Variation:
Add chopped coriander leaves during final stage of cooking.

A good accompaniment with: *Rice*

Serves: 6

Chhanar Kalia

Curried Cottage Cheese

250 gms chhana or panir
4 potatoes, quartered
1 onion, halved and sliced fine*
1 onion, ground to a paste*
½ tablespoon turmeric paste
1 tablespoon ginger paste
4 tablespoons ghee
4 tablespoons dahi
2–3 bay leaves
1 teaspoon garam masala paste
  (see page 7)
2 cups water
salt to taste
½ teaspoon sugar

* optional

Cut the *chhana* into inch squares and fry till lightly browned. Keep aside.

Fry the potatoes till lightly browned and keep aside.

Add bay leaves to the *ghee* in *karai* and after stirring, add sliced onion. Fry onion till brown. Then add all the *masala* pastes except *garam masala*. Stir-fry, sprinkling with water until *masalas* are cooked.

Add the *dahi* blended with ¼ cup water. Stir and cook until *dahi* is absorbed into *masalas*. Add 1½ cups water, salt and sugar to taste. Stir and bring to boil. Add potatoes. Cover and simmer until potatoes are three-quarters done. Add the *chhana* squares. Stir and simmer until potatoes are cooked. Stir in the *garam masala* paste. Simmer for 5 minutes and remove from fire.

A good accompaniment with: *Rice, Luchi, Ghee Bhat* or *Porota*

Serves: 4

Enchorer Kalia

Green Jackfruit Curry

500–750 gms green jackfruit
2 onions, halved and sliced fine
2 onions ground to a paste
1½ tablespoons turmeric
2 teaspoons chilli paste
1 tablespoon ginger paste
2–3 tablespoons dahi
3–4 bay leaves
garam masala (see page 7)
3 tablespoons ghee
salt to taste
1–2 teaspoons sugar
2 cups water

Peel the green jackfruit and prepare as directed under *Enchorer Dalna*. However, cut the jackfruit into larger chunks similar in size to meat for meat curry. Boil in water to cover for 15 minutes. Drain and keep aside.

Heat *ghee* in pan or *karai*. Add bay leaves and *garam masala* and fry for 2 minutes. Add sliced onion and fry till well browned but soft. Add all the *masala* pastes including the onion paste. Stir well and fry for 7–10 minutes. Sprinkle a little water. Add the jackfruit. Stir into the *masalas* and fry several minutes. Add the *dahi* after beating slightly. Stir in with the jackfruit and *masalas*. Stir and fry another 5 minutes and then add 1½ to 2 cups water. Add salt and sugar.

Cover and simmer over medium heat stirring from time to time until the water is reduced and there is approximately a cup or so of gravy in the pan.

A good accompaniment with: *Ghee Bhat, Luchi, Porota* or *Rice*

Serves: 8

Jhingé Chingri (1)

Ridge Gourd cooked with Shrimps

1 kg jhingé or tori
250 gms shrimps, peeled, cleaned
  and washed
½ tablespoon turmeric paste
1½ tablespoons coriander paste
1 tablespoon cummin paste
1 teaspoon chilli paste
salt and sugar
4–5 green chillies, slit
2 tablespoons oil
1 tablespoon ghee
4 bay leaves
½ teaspoon whole cummin seeds
1 tablespoon green coriander leaves
  (optional), chopped

Peel and slice *jhingé* in half lengthwise and slice quarter inch thick. Add half teaspoon salt and set aside for a while. Squeeze out all water drawn out by the salt.

Heat the oil in a *karai* and add *jhingé*. Cover and simmer for 5 minutes when *jhingé* will give out some water. Add the *masala* pastes and cook over brisk fire until water is reduced considerably.

Add the raw shrimps and green chillies and continue cooking till quite dry and oil comes to the surface. Adjust seasoning, adding a little sugar if preferred.

Separately fry the bay leaves and whole cummin seeds in the *ghee* and pour onto *Jhingé Chingri*. At the same time add the chopped coriander leaves. Stir well and remove from fire.

Microwave method
Squeeze out all the water drawn out by the salt from the *jhingé*. In a suitable dish with lid, mix together *jhingé*, *masala* pastes, salt and sugar cook on high power for 10 mins. Remove lid stir in green chillies and cook on medium power for another 10 mins. Stir in raw shrimps and cook on high power for 4 mins, let stand for 5 mins—follow as above

A good accompaniment with: *Rice, Luchi, Ghee Bhat* or *Porota*

Serves: 4–6

Jhingé Chingri (2)

Ridge Gourd Cooked with Shrimps

1 kg jhingé or tori
250 gms shrimps, peeled, cleaned
    and washed
3 potatoes, halved and
    sliced ¼ inch thick
2 onions, halved and sliced fine
¼ tablespoon turmeric paste
1 teaspoon chilli paste
1¼ teaspoons ginger paste
4 green chillies, cut in pieces
¼ fresh coconut, grated
4 tablespoons ghee
4 bay leaves
½–1 teaspoon salt
Sugar to taste

After adding a pinch of turmeric and salt, lightly fry the shrimps in oil and keep aside.

To the same pan add the *jhingé* and half to one teaspoon of salt. Cover and cook for 5 minutes. The *jhingé* will have given out a lot of water. Gauge the time and water required to cook the potatoes and accordingly add potatoes to the pan so that when potatoes are cooked, the pan will be nearly dry.

With the potatoes add the sliced onion, the *masala* pastes and green chillies. When potatoes are nearly done, add the grated coconut and the shrimps, taste for salt and add a little sugar. Cook until there is no gravy left.

Heat a tablespoon of *ghee*, fry the bay leaves and pour over *Jhingé Chingri*. Stir and remove from fire.

A good accompaniment with: *Rice* or *Luchi*

Serves: 6–8

Kumro Chingri

Red Pumpkin cooked with Shrimps

500 gms red pumpkin, diced fine
100 gms shrimps, cleaned and
shelled
3 tablespoons oil
3 tablespoons coriander paste
1½ tablespoons cummin paste
1½ teaspoons turmeric paste
1 teaspoon chilli paste
⅛ teaspoon panch phoran
2 bay leaves
salt and sugar to taste

Heat 2 tablespoons oil in a *karai*. First lightly fry the shrimps. Remove and keep aside. Add the diced pumpkin and salt. Stir. Cover and cook for 5 minutes. Remove cover. The pumpkin will have given out some water. Stir and cook another 5 minutes. Then add all the *masala* pastes, stir and cook until oil comes to the surface. Add the fried shrimps and mix well.

Heat the balance one spoon of oil in a frying pan. Add the bay leaves and *panch phoran*. When spluttering stops, pour over the contents of the *karai*. Stir and remove from fire.

Microwave method
In a suitable dish mix together diced pumpkin, salt, sugar and *masala* pastes cover with lid and cook on high for 6–8 mins. Stir in raw shrimps and cook on medium power for another 10 mins. Let it stand for 5 mins–follow as above.

A good accompaniment with: *Rice* or *Luchi*

Serves: 4–6

Lau Chingri

Marrow cooked with Shrimps

1 kg lau or dudhi, peeled, slit in
4 lengthwise, hard seeds
removed and then diced fine
1 cup peeled shrimps—fried in oil
for 5 minutes
2 tablespoons coriander paste
1 tablespoon cummin paste
¼ teaspoon turmeric paste
¼ teaspoon chilli paste
6 green chillies, slit
salt and sugar to taste
2–3 tablespoons oil
1 tablespoon ghee
2 bay leaves
garam masala (see page 7)

Heat oil to smoking hot in a *karai*. Add the *lau*, mix with oil in pan. Stir in 1 teaspoon salt, cover *karai* tightly and simmer covered for about 5 minutes. Now remove cover. There should be quite a lot of water from the *lau* in the *karai*. Add all the *masala* paste,s mix thoroughly and continue cooking over high heat for at least another 5–7 minutes, stirring from time to time.

The next stage of cooking depends on the amount of water the *lau* has given off. If there is a lot of water, continue cooking over high heat until nearly all the water is absorbed and the *lau* cooked. If there is not too much water after the first stage of cooking, reduce heat to a mild simmer, cover the *karai* (removing cover only from time to time to stir *lau*) and cook until *lau* is done. You will have to gauge for yourself how much water should cook the *lau*—which naturally depends on the condition of the *lau*, etc. The main point is that to get the best flavour, additional water should not be used.

When the *lau* is nearly dry, add the fried shrimp and the green chillies. Adjust the salt and add a little sugar to taste. Mix well and cook, stirring from time to time, until all the water is absorbed and oil comes to the surface.

In a separate pan, heat the *ghee* and add bay leaves and *garam masala*. Fry till *garam masala* stops spluttering and then pour *ghee*, *garam masala* and bay leaves over *Lau Chingri*. Stir and remove from fire.

Variations:
It makes a change to add a couple of small tomatoes chopped to the *masalas* for *Lau Chingri*.

Another variation, particularly popular with the East Bengali, is the addition of a fistful of chopped coriander leaves during the final stages of cooking.

A good accompaniment with: *Rice, Ghee Bhat* or *Luchi*

Serves: 6

Palong Chingri
Spinach with Prawns

1/2 kg palong (spinach)
1/4 kg medium sized prawns,
    cleaned and shell removed,
    but head and tails intact.
1 medium sized brinjal, diced
2 potatoes, diced without
    removing skin
4 inch piece of pumpkin, diced
    also with skin (approx 150
    gms)
1 onion, halved and sliced fine
4–6 green chillies, stems removed
    and slit
1 tablespoon oil
1/4 teaspoon of panch phoran
1 1/2 teaspoons chilli paste
1 tablespoon coriander paste
1 1/2 to 2 tablespoons cummin paste
1 tablespoon ginger paste
1 teaspoon garlic paste
salt and sugar to taste
4 bay leaves
1 tablespoon ghee

Rub prawns with a little turmeric paste and salt. Heat oil in pan and fry prawns for about 5 minutes or until just done. Remove from pan.

Add the *panch phoran* to the pan and when this begins to splutter, add the cleaned spinach and the salt. Stir. Cover pan and leave for about 5 minutes. Remove cover from pan. Add all the *masala* pastes. Stir thoroughly and continue cooking for a few minutes.

Then add the onion and all the diced vegetables and again stir well. Cover pan and continue cooking for about 12–15 minutes. Remove cover from pan. By this time all the vegetables should be nearly cooked and there should be barely any gravy in the pan.

Add the fried prawns and continue cooking another 5 minutes, stirring all the time so that it does not catch at the bottom. Remove when nearly dry. In a *karai*, heat 1 teaspoon of *ghee*. Add a couple of bay leaves when *ghee* is hot and pour in the spinach. Mix well. Remove from fire.

Microwave method
Chop spinach. In a suitable dish with lid, mix together spinach, brinjal, potatoes, pumpkin, onion slices and salt. Cover and cook on high for 10 mins. Remove lid, stir in *masala* pastes, sugar and cook on medium for another 12 mins or till vegetables are almost done. Add raw prawns and cook on high for another 4 mins. Let it stand for 5 mins. In a pan heat 1 teaspoon *ghee*, add *pach phoran* and bay leaves, when spluttering stops, add it to the spinach and prawns. Mix well and serve.

A good accompaniment with: *Rice*

Serves: 4–6

Thor, Mocha O Kanchkola
The Banana Plant

The Bengalis utilise each and every part of the banana plant. Apart from eating the ripe bananas, they make succulent and special dishes from the pith of the plant called *thor* (available only from a banana plant which has flowered), the flower—*mocha* and the green or unripe banana—*kanchkola*. The banana leaves are utlised to cover and seal various vegetables and fish preparations which are then steamed or boiled in water or baked. The leaves were, and still are, utilised in lieu of plates for eating. It is still traditional to use them at weddings—an excellent and perhaps the easiest disposable plate. Eco-friendly as well.

Thor

Banana Pith

The pith or *thor* of the banana is layered, round, white and compact and is sold in the bazaars of Calcutta and Bengal in 18 or 24 inch lengths. The ones to buy are those which if you press your thumb nail into the skin, it goes in easily. A 18–24 inch piece after cooking reduces considerably and should feed 3–4 persons.

Preparation:
Oil your hands and fingers thoroughly before cutting *thor*. As you chop, a sticky juice exudes which can stain fingers rather badly.

Remove the outer layer of pith. Then chop the *thor* as you would onions, into very, very fine circles.

Collect 4 or 5 of these circles together and once again chop these into very, very fine julienne strips.

Continue until all the *thor* is chopped.

Take 2 teaspoons salt, half teaspoon turmeric and mix into chopped *thor*. Leave for half an hour, by which time some liquid should have been drawn out.

Mix the *thor* as you would dough, and then finally squeeze by hand to eliminate all liquid and remove to another dish.

Throw away liquid accumulated in first dish.

The *thor* is now ready for cooking.

Note: If preferred, the *thor* can now be boiled in water for 10 minutes, drained and made ready for cooking.

Thor Chenchki

Curried Banana Pith

*18–24 inch length thor,
    prepared as directed*
1/8 teaspoon mustard seeds
1/2 fresh coconut, grated
1 teaspoon turmeric paste
3 teaspoons mustard paste
1/2 teaspoon chilli paste
4–6 green chillies, slit
1 tablespoon mustard oil

Heat oil and when very hot, add mustard seeds and let this cook a few minutes until it stops spluttering. Add *thor*, stir and add all the *masalas*. Stir. Cover pan and cook 5 minutes. Remove lid and keep frying the *thor*.

A succulent *thor* should cook in its own juice without addition of any extra water, but if you find the mixture dry and the vegetable not quite done and tending to burn, add half cup water and continue cooking until the water is practically all absorbed. Add green chillies, grated coconut (keeping a little for garnish) stir into the vegetables. Remove from heat and place on serving dish, sprinkling the remaining coconut over it.

Note: SHOULD NOT BE RE-HEATED

Variations:
Thor Chingri: Separately fry 250 gms cleaned shrimps in a little oil. Add to *thor* along with green chillies, etc. Continue cooking as above.

Microwave method
Boil *thor* and drain. In a suitable dish with lid, mix *thor,* 1 tablespoon oil, *masala* pastes, salt and sugar. Cook on high for 6–8 mins. Remove cover and stir in three-quarters grated coconut, raw shrimps and green chillies. Mix well and cook on medium for 10 mins. Let it stand for 5 mins. In a pan heat 1 teaspoon oil and the mustard seeds, let them splutter, pour over *Thor Chingri*. Mix well. Add remaining coconut and serve.

A good accompaniment with: *Rice*

Serves: 4–6

Thorer Ghanto

Dry Spiced Banana Pith

*12 inch length thor, prepared
    as directed*
2 tablespoons coriander paste
*2 tablespoons chola (whole gram),
    soaked in water overnight to
    soften*
2 tablespoons ginger paste
1 tablespoon cummin paste
*6–8 green chillies chopped into
    large pieces*
*1 teaspoon garam masala paste
    or powder*
2–3 tablespoons oil
1 tablespoon ghee
4 bay leaves
salt and sugar to taste
2 tablespoons milk
1/4 cup water

Place *thor* in pan with a small amount of water. Boil for about 15–20 minutes. Pour into colander to drain water. Squeeze out any excess water. Heat oil in pan till smoking hot. Add the *masala* pastes (except *garam masala*) and cook for a few minutes. Add the *thor*, mix well and keep frying until *thor* is quite dry.

Add quarter cup water, *chola*, *garam masala*, green chillies, salt and sugar to taste. Mix, adjust heat to a mild simmer, and continue cooking, stirring from time to time. When the water is absorbed, add 2 tablespoons milk and stir into *thor*. Remove pan from fire.

Place a separate pan on the fire, add *ghee* and when hot, fry bay leaves in this for a couple of minutes. Pour hot *ghee* and bay leaves over *thor*. Bring the pan with *thor* back on the fire.

Stir the *ghee* in well, cook over high heat for a couple of minutes. Add the *garam masala* paste or powder. Stir and remove from fire.

A good accompaniment with: *Rice*

Serves: 4–6

Method of preparing the Banana Flower

I remember a friend of my mother's telling me the crisis that befell her when, as a new bride, her mother-in-law sat her down to cut the vegetable and said to her: "To begin with, cut the *mocha*." The young bride had never cut *mocha* in her life! She looked at it from all angles and then decided to chop right through the *mocha*.

Luckily for her, the *mali* (gardener) working nearby had been watching her and realising that she did not know one end of the *mocha* from the other, told her how to go about things and saved the day for her!

Mocha is the flower or spadix of the banana plant. The type commonly found in the market is the end portion of the spadix which is chopped off after the bananas have been formed. It is purple in colour. The other variety, not so commonly sold and more expensive, is the *mocha*, larger and greener, which is cut from the banana tree before any fruit has matured. The second variety is better tasting. However, either variety can be cooked.

The purple or green leaves of the spadix are inedible. Only the inner immature banana fruit is eaten and even then, care must be taken to remove the stylus.

Oil your hands before preparing *mocha*. The *mocha* has a gummy substance which can stain the fingers.

Peel off one leaf at a time. Remove the long stick-like immature bananas. Chop off ⅛ inch of the top portion bearing the stylus and discard it. Chop what is left and soak in a bowl of water kept handy for this purpose.

Continue peeling leaves off the *mocha* and chopping as directed until you come to the portion of the spadix which has barely any fruit—discard this.

Remember to oil your hands as and when necessary when cutting the *mocha*.

Drain the water in which the *mocha* has been soaking.

Place *mocha* in a suitable sized pan, cover with water, boil for about 15 minutes. Remove from fire and drain off the water.

Squeeze *mocha* with fingers and get rid of excess water.

The *mocha* is now ready for cooking.

Mochar Ghanto

Dry Spiced Banana Flower

1 mocha, prepared as directed
  and boiled
2 tablespoons dry whole chola
  (whole chick-peas), soaked in
  water overnight to soften
2 tablespoons coriander paste
3–4 tablespoons cummin paste
1 tablespoon turmeric paste
¼ teaspoon chilli paste (optional)
6–8 green chillies, slit
2 tablespoons ginger paste
3–4 tablespoons oil
1 tablespoon ghee
4 bay leaves
garam masala, whole (see page 7)
2 tablespoons milk
¼ cup water
1 teaspoon garam masala, paste
  or powder
a fistful of grated coconut
6 boris, fried crisp and broken up
  coarsely with a rolling pin
2 teaspoons sugar
1 teaspoon salt

Heat mustard oil in pan till smoking hot. Add all the masala pastes and fry for a few minutes (approximately 5 minutes).

Add the mocha, mix well with spices in the pan and continue cooking, stirring all the while.

When the mixture begins to catch at the bottom of the pan, add quarter cup water and reduce heat to a mild simmer.

Now add the chola, green chillies, salt to taste and 2 teaspoons of sugar. Continue stirring and cooking until all the water is absorbed. Then add the 2 tablespoons of milk, mix with the mocha and remove from the fire.

Place a frying pan on the fire and add 1 tablespoon of ghee. When hot, add the bay leaves and garam masala and cook for a couple of minutes. Now take the contents and pour over the mocha.

Return pan with mocha to fire and cook for a few minutes.

Finally add the garam masala paste or powder and remove from fire.

Pour into serving dish and sprinkle first coconut and then the bori over mocha.

A good accompaniment with: Rice

Serves: 6

Mochar Paturi

Banana Flower smoked in Banana Leaf

½ kg mocha, prepared as
    directed and boiled
2 teaspoons mustard paste
1 tablespoon poppy seed, ground
    to paste
½ teaspoon turmeric paste
¼ teaspoon chilli paste
8–10 chopped green chillies
banana leaves
130 gms or 1 teacup mustard oil

Squeeze out as much water as possible from the mocha.

Mix the mustard, poppy seed, turmeric and chilli pastes plus the chopped green chillies. Finally add the mustard oil and mix well again,, adding salt to taste.

Heat an iron *tawa* or griddle on the fire and on this place on top of each other, cross-wise, 4 to 5 suitable sized banana leaves.

Place the *mocha* on the leaves and cook until the oil oozes out from the sides or until nearly all the banana leaves are scorched through leaving only the one nearest the *mocha*.

Remove *mocha* on unscorched banana leaf to a serving platter.

Microwave method
In a suitable dish with lid place a banana leaf. Mix together *mocha*, oil, *masala* pastes, green chillies, salt and sugar. Place in the dish on the banana leaf. Place another banana leaf on top and tuck in the sides to make a parcel. Cook on medium power for 10 mins. Remove lid, turn the parcel over and cook on medium power for another 15 mins. Let it stand for 4 mins. Serve from the banana leaf.

A good accompaniment with: *Rice*

Serves: 6–8

Preparation of Kanchkola

Preparation of Raw Green Bananas

Peel green bananas. Cut crosswise into 1½ inch to 2 inch slices. Rub bananas with a pinch of turmeric and some salt. Place in a pan with water to cover. Boil until bananas are cooked and quite soft. Drain off water.

Kanchkolar Cutlet

Green Banana Cutlets

6 raw green bananas
2 onions, either ground to a paste
  or chopped fine
1 tablespoon ginger paste
1 teaspoon turmeric paste
1 teaspoon chilli paste
3 medium tomatoes, skinned and
  chopped
2 tablespoons ghee
also ghee for frying cutlets
½ teaspoon sugar
salt to taste

Peel and boil bananas as directed and mash to pulp.

Heat *ghee* in pan. Add the onion, ginger, turmeric and chilli pastes. Mix well and fry 3 or 5 minutes. Add skinned, chopped tomatoes, and finally the banana pulp. Mix thoroughly adding salt and sugar to taste.

Remove from fire when mixture has browned and appears cooked. Cool. Divide mixture into 12 portions and shape into cutlets quarter-inch thick. Heat *ghee* in frying pan and fry cutlets until well browned on both sides. Remove and drain off oil.

Note: If banana mixture is too soft after cooking, sprinkle with a little flour to stiffen.

The cutlets may also be coated in egg flour mixture and bread crumbs and fried.

A good accompaniment with: *Rice* or by itself with sliced *onion* and *tomatoes*.

Serves: 6

Kanchkolar Cutlet Curry

Curried Green Banana Cutlets

12 kanchkolar cutlets, fried
1 coconut, grated and steeped in
    2 cups hot water to produce 2
    cups coconut milk (see general
    instruction page 8)
4 green chillies, chopped
salt and sugar to taste
2 limes
1 tablespoon cummin, dry-fried
    and powdered

Approximately 20 minutes before the meal is to be served, bring coconut milk to a brisk boil in a large pan. Continue cooking the milk over a hot fire for about 10 minutes or until it is thick and creamy. Add salt, sugar and green chillies and then slip in the banana cutlets. Cook for another 10 minutes or so. Remove from fire, and squeeze lime juice over cutlets.

Finally, remove to serving dish and dry-fried sprinkle cummin powder.

A good accompaniment with: *Rice, Luchi* or *Ghee Bhat*

Serves: 6

Doi Begun

Brinjals with Yogurt

500 gms small round brinjals, cut
    in four lengthwise
a pinch of turmeric paste
oil for frying brinjals
2 tablespoons pure ghee or butter
250 gms or 1 cup dahi
½ teaspoon chilli powder
    (optional)
2 tablespoons cummin seeds, dry-
    fried and powdered
salt to taste
½ teaspoon sugar

Rub the turmeric and a little salt on the brinjals. Fry in hot oil until well browned. Drain off oil.

In a *karai*, heat 2 tablespoons *ghee*. Add the fried brinjals. Whip together the salt, sugar and *dahi* and add to the pan. Stir and mix well. Cook for 10 minutes over a mild flame. Before removing from fire, sprinkle with dry-fried powdered cummin.

Note: Do not reheat.

A good accompaniment with: *Rice*

Serves: 4–6

Doi Potol

Parwals cooked with Yogurt

1 kg potol or parwal
2 medium sized onions
1 tablespoon ginger paste
1 tablespoon turmeric paste
1½ teaspoons chilli paste
3–4 tablespoons coriander paste
2 tablespoons cummin paste
140 gms dahi, lightly blended in
   1 cup water
2 teaspoons sugar or less if
   preferred
salt to taste
3 tablespoons ghee
4 tablespoons mustard oil or
   vegetable oil
garam masala, whole (see page 7)
2 bay leaves

Cut the ends off the *potol* and peel skin in strips, giving the *potol* a striped effect.

Heat mustard or vegetable oil in pan and fry *potol* over high heat until lightly browned. Remove *potol* from pan with slotted spoon, draining off as much oil as possible.

In the same pan add the *ghee* to the oil in pan and when quite hot add *garam masala* and bay leaves and fry for few minutes. Then add sliced onions, continue frying till onions are golden brown. Add ground *masala* pastes and fry for 5 minutes taking care that *masalas* do not stick to the pan. Add a few drops of water if necessary. Add the *dahi* and water and let it come to a simmer.

Add fried *potols*, sugar and salt to taste. Increase the heat until it comes to the boil. Then reduce heat and cook about 20 minutes.

The *Doi Potol* is ready when there is a thick gravy and the *ghee* has come to the surface.

A good accompaniment with: *Rice, Luchi, Ghee Bhat* or *Porota*

Serves: 8–12

Dolmas

Stuffed Vegetables

As far as I know, the word *dolma* is not used anywhere else in India. The word is obviously either of Greek or Turkish origin, but how it came into the Bengali cuisine I do not know, except that recent excavations now prove that when Alexander the Great conquered India, he did come as far as what is today known as Bengal.

I have put *dolmas* together with the vegetable recipes.

In Bengal, *dolma* means a stuffed vegetable as it would in either Greece or Turkey. The most popular vegetable for *Dolma* in Bengal is *potol* or *parwal*, although other vegetables are used, including cucumber and cabbage.

The stuffing can be made of meat, fish, shrimps, *chhana* or *dal*.

Potoler Dolma

Stuffed Parwals

For making *dolmas*, scrape the *parwal* gently with either a knife or scraper. Cut ¼ inch slice across from one end and retain this piece.

Carefully remove seeds inside with either a salt spoon or hairpin.

Stuff with prawn or fish stuffing.

Replace the cut bit, passing a toothpick through the vegetable to close or make a little thick paste with water and flour and seal ends with this mixture.

Heat oil or *ghee* in pan for deep frying until blue haze appears. Fry *dolmas* a few at a time until *parwals* are browned.

Remove and drain oil.

Keep warm until time to serve. Should not be fried too far in advance as they are inclined to become soggy when left too long.

Chingri Dolma

Prawn Dolma

1 kg or 18–20 parwals, prepared
   for stuffing
½ kg prawns, cleaned and
   chopped
1–2 green chillies (optional),
   chopped into small pieces
1 tablespoon ginger paste
1 teaspoon turmeric paste
1 teaspoon chilli paste
1 teaspoon garlic paste
1 teaspoon garam masala paste
2 tablespoons ghee
salt to taste
4–6 onions, chopped
50 gms ginger, chopped

Heat *ghee* over high flame and add onions. Fry onions till just turning brown. Add *masalas* and fry a couple of minutes, then add raw prawns. Continue frying. Reduce heat to medium and if too dry, sprinkle with a little water. Add chopped ginger and green chillies. The prawns should be cooked for approximately 15 minutes and the mixture should be slightly moist. Add *garam masala*, mix thoroughly and remove from heat.

Stuff *parwals* with mixture, sealing ends as directed.

Deep fry till skin of *parwal* is lightly browned and crisp.

A good accompaniment with: *Luchi*

Serves: 8–10

Fish Dolma

1 kg or 18–20 parwals, prepared
    for stuffing
300 gms any large fish—with few
    bones, i.e. rahu, bekti or
    pomfret
1 cup water
½ onion
½ inch piece ginger, chopped
2 cloves garlic, chopped
masala pastes, as for prawn
    dolma

Boil fish in a cup of water, adding a few pieces of chopped ginger, onion and 2 cloves chopped garlic. When done, drain fish into colander but retain fish stock.

Remove skin and bones and mash fish together with the onion, ginger and garlic in which fish was boiled. Heat *ghee* in pan and cook *masala* as for *Prawn Dolmas*. Add fish, chopped ginger and green chillies. Fry fish sprinkling with fish stock as and when necessary. Finally add *garam masala*.

The fish should be a smooth, slightly moist paste. Remove pan from heat.

Stuff *parwals* and fry as for *Prawn Dolmas*.

A good accompaniment with: *Luchi*

Serves: 8–10

Dolma Curry

18–20 prawn or fish dolmas unfried
2 onions, ground to a paste
3 onions, halved and finely sliced
1 tablespoon turmeric paste
1 teaspoon chilli paste
200 gms dahi
2–3 cups water
1½ teaspoons salt
1½ teaspoons sugar
4 tablespoons ghee
garam masala, whole (see page 7)
2 bay leaves

Heat *ghee* in largish pan, add bay leaves and *garam masala*. Fry for a couple of minutes. Add sliced onions, and fry till golden brown but still soft. Then add onion paste, turmeric and chilli paste and fry the *masalas* sprinkling with a little water if necessary.

Mix *dahi* in the remaining water and pour onto fried *masalas*.

Bring to the boil.

Add the *dolmas*, placing them if possible, in one layer in the pan. Simmer gently for 30 minutes. The water should be reduced to half by this time.

Remove from heat.

Care must be taken while *dolmas* are cooking to see that they do not stick to the bottom of the pan.

Shake gently from time to time, turning carefully only once.

Variation: Baked Dolmas
Fry onions, cook *masalas*, add *dahi* but reduce quantity of water to 1½ cups, let it come to the boil, remove from heat. In a large oven-proof dish, place stuffed *dolmas*, preferably in a single layer. Pour gravy over *dolmas*. Cover dish with aluminium foil, sealing edge. Bake in 325°F and cook for 5 minutes. Remove. Serve direct from oven-proof dish. Can be rewarmed by sprinkling water and placing in oven preheated to 325°F for 5 minutes.

A good accompaniment with: *Any cereal*

Serves: 8–10

Mangshor Dolmas

Parwals stuffed with Minced Mutton

1 kg (18–20) parwals
400 gms mutton minced very fine
4 onions, minced fine
½ teaspoon turmeric paste
½ teaspoon black pepper, freshly
   ground
½ teaspoon chilli paste
½ teaspoon garlic paste
1 teaspoon garam masala,
   powdered
1 tablespoon raisins, cleaned and
   soaked in water
salt and sugar to taste
2 tablespoons ghee or oil for cooking mince
oil or ghee for frying dolmas

Prepare *parwals* as instructed in *Potoler Dolma*. Keep *parwals* aside.

In a pan heat 2 tablespoons *ghee* or oil.

Add minced meat and fry until it changes colour.

Add the *masala* pastes, salt and sugar to taste, freshly ground pepper and the minced onions. Stir and fry until onions and meat are quite cooked and oil rises to the surface.

Add raisins. Mix well. Add the *garam masala*, stir and fry a couple of minutes and remove from fire.

Stuff the prepared *parwals* with the mince.

Replace cut end of *parwals* after filling by either sticking in place with a toothpick or flour and water.

Fill a *karai* two-thirds full with oil. Heat till smoking hot.

Fry the stuffed *parwals* a few at a time until skin of *parwal* is lightly browned and crisp.

Remove with slotted spoon and drain on paper before serving.

A good accompaniment with: *Any cereal*

Serves: 8–10

Mangshor Dolma Curry (1)
Stuffed Parwal Curry

18–20 mutton dolmas, unfried
3 onions, halved and sliced fine
2 onions, ground to a paste
1 tablespoon turmeric paste
1 teaspoon chilli paste
6–8 tablespoon dahi
2–3 cups water
salt and sugar to taste
4 tablespoons ghee
garam masala, whole (see page 7)
4 bay leaves

Heat *ghee* in a *karai* or a large flat pan with sides.

Add bay leaves and *garam masala* and fry till spluttering stops. Add the sliced onion, stir-fry until turned brown but still soft.

Add the onion, turmeric and chilli pastes and stir-fry until *masalas* appear cooked. Sprinkle water if too dry.

Mix *dahi* with the water and pour onto fried *masalas* in pan through a sieve. Bring it to a boil.

Add the prepared *dolmas* placing them, if possible, in a single layer in the pan.

Simmer gently for 30 minutes. The water should be reduced to half by this time (It may be baked in a medium hot oven at this point).

Remove from heat.

Note: Care must be taken while *dolmas* are cooking to see that they do not stick to the bottom of the pan. Shake pan carefully from time to time turning *dolmas* over carefully once.

A good accompaniment with: *Any cereal*

Serves: 8–10

Ambal Tauk Achar, Chutney and Pickles

Nimki, Shingara and Kochuri

Murgi Cutlet (Chicken)

Elish Fry

Aam Jhol and Macher Dimer Taur

Mangshor Gota Moshla and Mangshor Curry

Tel Muri, Chire Bhaja and Alu Kabli

Brinjal Vindaloo (Alternative to Pork Vindaloo)

Mangshor Dolma Curry (2)

Cabbage Leaves stuffed with Mutton and Curried

The dolmas:
16 large cabbage leaves
400 gms mince mutton
4 medium onions, minced fine
1 teaspoon turmeric paste
1 tablespoon ginger paste
½ teaspoon garlic paste
½ teaspoon chilli paste or freshly
*   ground pepper*
1 tablespoon raisins, cleaned and
*   soaked in water*
1 teaspoon garam masala, powder
*   or paste*
1 tablespoon green coriander
*   leaves (optional), chopped*
salt and sugar to taste
2 tablespoon ghee or oil
string or thread for tying dolmas

The curry:
1 onion, halved and sliced fine
2 onions, ground to a paste
1 tablespoon turmeric paste
1 teaspoon chilli paste
4 tomatoes, chopped
2–3 cups water
4 tablespoons ghee
garam masala, whole (see page 7)
4 bay leaves

Parboil the cabbage leaves for 5 minutes. Drain and dry on towel.

Heat *ghee* or oil in pan. Add mince, stir-fry until mince changes colour.

Add minced onions and fry 5 minutes.

Add the *masala* pastes including chilli or freshly ground pepper, as preferred. Stir-fry until meat and *masalas* are quite cooked and oil comes to the surface of the pan. Sprinkle water, if necessary.

Add raisins and mix. Then add *garam masala*. Stir-fry for 5 minutes and remove from fire. At this point coriander leaves may be added.

Spread a cabbage leaf flat. Place a tablespoon or more of filling about half-inch from the wider end of the leaf. Level filling an inch wide across the leaf leaving an edge of about three-quarter inch on both sides.

Fold over the wider portion of leaf left bare (half inch) Fold over once more to cover the mince. Then fold in from two sides the portion of the leaf without filling. Hold in place and roll cabbage leaf into compact roll.

Tie rolls crosswise with thread to keep from opening during cooking.

Heat *ghee* in a *karai* or large flat pan with sides.

Add bay leaves and *garam masala* and fry till spluttering stops.

Add sliced onion and fry to a gold brown.

Add all the *masala* pastes and stir-fry until *masalas* are cooked. Sprinkle water, if necessary.

Add chopped tomatoes and cook until tomatoes are blended in with *masalas*.

Add water and bring to the boil.

Add salt and sugar to taste. Stir.

Reduce heat and simmer gently.

Slide in prepared cabbage *dolmas*.

Cook until cabbage is quite soft and gravy reduced by half.

Remove from fire.

To serve, heat *Domla Curry,* if necessary. Remove *dolmas* to serving dish with slotted spoon. Cut away and remove string.

Pour hot gravy over.

Note: Prawns or shrimps may be substituted for the minced meat.

A good accompaniment with: Any *cereal*

Serves: 6–8

Chhanar Dolma

Parwals stuffed with Cottage Cheese

8–10 large parwals prepared for stuffing
250–300 gms chhana or cottage cheese, freshly prepared
3 chopped onions
1¼ tablespoons turmeric paste
1½ teaspoons chilli powder
1" piece ginger, chopped very fine
1 tablespoon ginger, ground
6 tablespoons dahi
salt and sugar to taste
3 tablespoons ghee or oil
bay leaves
garam masala, whole (see page 7)
1½ cups water

Heat 1 tablespoon *ghee* or oil and fry 2 chopped onions till just turning brown. Add quarter teaspoon turmeric paste; half teaspoon chilli paste and the finely chopped ginger. Stir-fry the *masalas* until cooked—a couple of minutes—sprinkling water while cooking, as necessary.

Add the *chhana* or *panir*, salt and sugar to taste. Stir and cook mixing in the *chhana* with the *masalas*. Cook for 5 minutes and remove from fire. Keep aside.

Stuff each *parwal* with some of the prepared *chhana*.

Replace cut end of *parwal* after filling either by sticking in place with a toothpick or with a little paste (thick) made of flour and water.

Heat the remaining 2 tablespoons of *ghee* or oil in a *karai* or shallow pan. Add the bay leaves and *garam masala*. When spluttering stops add the remaining turmeric and chilli pastes and the ground ginger paste. Stir-fry for 5 minutes, sprinkling with water if necessary.

Blend together the 6 tablespoons *dahi* and 1½ cups water. Add to the *masalas* along with salt and sugar to taste. Stir well and gently simmer for 5 minutes.

Now add the prepared stuffed *parwals* in one layer to the pan. Spoon gravy over the *parwals* and continue to simmer gently until the *parwals* are cooked. Remove from fire.

A good accompaniment with: *Rice, Luchi* or *Ghee Bhat*

Serves: 4–6

MAACH

FISH

Maach

Fish

A Bengali meal without fish is incomplete.

Besides the *Maacher Jhol* about which I have written later, there are innumerable fish recipes originating both in East and West Bengal.

Bengalis believe that the flavour of river fish can be best appreciated if it is cooked with mustard oil. To some, mustard oil has too strong a flavour. This can be considerably reduced if the oil is properly heated before use. For some of my guests who do not like mustard oil, I have served fish preparations made in other vegetable oils after 'burning' the oil thoroughly, and the results have been satisfactory.

(Burning: a term used to signify oil heated till smoking).

Bengali fish specialities are those generally cooked with mustard paste, *dahi* and also those which are steamed and/or baked. The banana leaf finds an important place in a number of fish preparations when it is used as a seal-jacket for baking, and imparts a delicious and delicate flavour.

Substitutes can be used for most of the fish mentioned in the recipes, with satisfactory results.

In this section I have also included two recipes for crab and one for turtle.

For the readers' convenience, the recipes for a particular variety of fish have been grouped together.

Maacher Jhol

Spiced Fish Stew

It will not be out of place to begin this chapter on fish with *Maacher Jhol*. The Bengali and his *Maacher Jhol* are synonymous to other Indians. Jokes are made about it and it is referred to with a certain derision. Despite this, it continues to be the first favourite with most Bengalis. *Jhol* is nothing more than a spiced stew and like that much maligned dish, it can be well made or otherwise turn out to taste like dishwater. However, a well cooked *jhol* is a delight.

The quantity of spices in a *jhol* can be increased or decreased at will. Thus it is served as one of the first solids to Bengali babies and also to invalids. The addition of sliced raw bananas to *jhol* is said to be particularly good for those suffering from dysentery. Boiled raw bananas are considered a very good 'binder' for the stomach.

During the long hot summer months *Maacher Jhol* and rice are eaten for the midday meal in most Bengali homes. Served tepidly warm or at room temperature, it is ideal for the hot summer days. *Rui* is the most popular fish for *jhol*, although *singhi*, *magoor* and *koi* (all bought live) come a close second. *Parshé* is also popular and the smaller variety of *bekti* is also used, as also some of the other small fish found in the bazars of Bengal. In Bombay, I have found *rawas* or *surmai* reasonable substitutes. Pomfret, however, has too distinctive a flavour for *jhol*.

Rui Maacher Jhol

Spiced Carp Stew

500 gms rui (rahu, carp)
3–4 potatoes, cut lengthwise into
4–6 pieces
½ tablespoon turmeric paste
1 tablespoon coriander paste
1 teaspoon cummin paste
a pinch or ⅛ teaspoon panch
  phoran
2 bay leaves
4 green chillies, slit (more if
  preferred)
salt to taste
¼ teaspoon chilli paste (optional)
6 tablespoons mustard oil
3–4 cups water

Cut the *Rui* into half inch thick slices approximately 2 inches × 1 inch or any preferred size. Rub the fish with a small quantity of the turmeric paste and sprinkle with a little salt.

Heat oil in *karai* or pan and fry fish sliced until just turning brown. Remove from *karai* with slotted spoon, draining away excess oil from fish. Then lightly fry potatoes in the same oil. Remove and drain.

Remove all but 1 tablespoon oil from *karai*, bring this to smoking hot, add the bay leaves and *panch phoran*.

When the *panch phoran* stops spluttering, add the turmeric, coriander and cummin pastes to the *karai* with the water. If chilli paste is being used, add now.

Bring to the boil, add fried potatoes and let it simmer for about 10 minutes and then add salt and green chillies.

After another 5 minutes add the fried fish to the *jhol* and cook another 10 minutes.

Remove from fire.

Variation:
Rui Maacher Alu Phulkopir Jhol

To the above recipe, add 1 medium sized cauliflower broken into flowerets. Fry cauliflower lightly along with potatoes.

Then follow cooking procedure for *Rui Maacher Jhol* adding quarter teaspoon chilli paste.

A good accompaniment with: *Rice*

Serves: 6

Maacher Sorsé Jhol

Fish Stew spiced with Mustard

250 gms white fleshed fish, rui,
    bekti or rawas, etc.
4 tablespoons mustard paste
1/4 teaspoon turmeric paste
1/4 teaspoon chilli paste
6–8 green chillies, slit
salt to taste
3 tablespoons mustard oil
3 cups water

Cut the fish into even pieces.

Mix together all the *masala* pastes in water in a bowl.

Heat oil to smoking and fry the pieces of fish in the oil for 3–5 minutes.

Pour the *masala*-water into the pan through a sieve. Add salt to taste and the green chillies. Let contents of the pan come to the boil.

Reduce heat and simmer gently for approximately 15 minutes or until fish is cooked.

A good accompaniment with: *Rice*

Serves: 4

Rui Maacher Curry

Carp Curry (1)

250 gms rui fish (any white-
    fleshed fish may be substituted)
4 potatoes, peeled and quartered
1 onion, halved and sliced fine
1/2 tablespoon turmeric paste
1 teaspoon chilli paste
1 teaspoon ginger paste
1/4 teaspoon garlic paste
1 onion, ground to a paste
4 bay leaves
garam masala (see page 7)
salt and sugar to taste
oil for frying fish and potatoes
2 tablespoons ghee

Cut fish into four large pieces.

Rub the fish with a little turmeric and salt and fry in smoking hot oil until lightly browned. Fry the potatoes in oil till just turning brown. Drain off oil from pan.

Heat the *ghee* in the same pan. Add bay leaves and *garam masala*.

Stir and fry a couple of minutes and then add the sliced onion. Fry till limp but quite brown.

Add all the *masala* pastes including onion.

Stir-fry adding a sprinkling of water as necessary until *masalas* look cooked and have changed colour.

Add 2 cups water, stir and add the fried potatoes. Cover and simmer until potatoes are two-thirds done.

Stir in the fish and simmer until both fish and potatoes are cooked and there is only a thick gravy in the pan.

A good accompaniment with: *Rice, Ghee Bhat*

Serves: 2–4

Rui Maacher Korma

Carp Curry with Yogurt

250 gms rui fish or any white-
*   fleshed fish*
1 tablespoon ginger paste
1 teaspoon chilli paste
1 onion, ground to paste
½ cup dahi
salt and sugar to taste
2 bay leaves
garam masala (see page 7)
2 onions, halved and sliced fine
2 tablespoons ghee

Cut the fish into 4 large pieces, wash and dry.

In a bowl mix together all the *masala* pastes, the *dahi*, salt and a little sugar and the fish. Cover and marinate for half an hour.

Heat *ghee* in pan till smoking. Add bay leaves and *garam masala*. Stir-fry a couple of minutes and then add the sliced onions. Fry onions, stirring from time to time, until quite brown.

Add the fish and *masala-dahi* mixture to pan. Stir and cover pan with tight fitting lid.

Reduce heat and simmer very gently until fish is cooked.

Remove cover from pan, stir and adjust seasoning. Remove from fire.

A good accompaniment with: *Rice, Ghee Bhat*

Serves: 4

Rui Maacher Kalia

Carp Curry (2)

250 gms rui fish
2 medium potatoes, halved
2 medium tomatoes, chopped
1 large onion paste
1 teaspoon chilli paste
1 teaspoon garam masala paste
1½ teaspoons turmeric paste
¼ teaspoon whole cummin seeds
2 bay leaves
1 tablespoon ghee
1½ teaspoon salt
½ teaspoons sugar
3 tablespoons oil
1½ cups water

Cut the fish into 4 pieces, wash and dry.

Rub half teaspoon salt and 1 teaspoon turmeric to fish and potatoes.

Heat oil in a pan and fry the fish and potatoes separatly till golden, remove and set aside.

Heat *ghee* in a pan, add the bayleaves and cummin seeds. Once the seeds stop spluttering, add onion, turmeric and chilli paste. Stir-fry *masalas* for 2–3 minutes.

Add chopped tomatoes and stir-fry for another 2 minutes or till the tomatoes turn pulpy.

Lower the heat and add *dahi*, stir-fry for another 2–3 minutes or until *dahi* is absorbed in the *masala*.

Add water and bring it to a boil, add the potatoes and simmer for about 3–4 minutes, add the fish and *garam masala* paste, simmer for another 3–4 minutes or until potatoes are cooked. Adjust seasoning. Remove from fire.

Serves: 4

Rui Maacher Doi Maach

Carp in Yogurt

4–6 large pieces rui fish or any
   white-fleshed fish
oil for frying fish
2–3 tablespoons ghee
2–3 bay leaves
1 onion, halved and minced
2 onions, pasted
½ tablespoon turmeric paste
2 teaspoons chilli paste
1 tablespoon ginger paste
⅛ teaspoon garlic paste (optional)
½ cup dahi, blended with 1 cup
   water
salt to taste
1–2 teaspoons sugar
6–8 green chillies, slit
a few raisins, soaked in water
garam masala (see page 7)

In hot oil fry the fish until just about to turn brown. Keep aside after draining well.

In a *karai* add *ghee* and when hot, the bay leaves and *garam masala*. Stir-fry for a couple of minutes, then add sliced onion. Fry, stirring from time to time, until onions turn brown but are still soft.

Add the onion paste and all the other *masala* pastes. Stir and fry till *masalas* change colour. Sprinkle with a little water as you fry *masalas*. Blending the *dahi* well with water, pour into *karai* through a sieve. Reduce temperature of the fire to a gentle simmer immediately.

Add salt, sugar and green chillies. Simmer, stirring for 5 minutes.

Add the fried fish, placing in one layer in the *karai*. Spoon gravy over fish. Sprinkle with raisins.

Simmer over very gentle fire, shaking *karai* from time to time, until fish is quite cooked, gravy has thickened and oil risen to the surface.

Note: Heat should be carefully controlled when cooking the fish; if cooked over high heat, the gravy will curdle. It is also difficult to stir the pan without breaking the fish during the final stages of cooking. Therefore, holding the *karai* by a handle, shake it so that the *masalas* cannot catch at the bottom.

A good accompaniment with: *Rice, Ghee Bhat*

Serves: 3–4

Pixie's Special

Steamed Fish with Green Peas and Yogurt

My sister Pixie is the cook of the family. When I say *cook* I mean someone who makes her own recipes. 'Pixie's Special' is one that she discovered.

To begin with, she decided to cook *Rui* with *Matarsuti*. But then she found she had some *dahi*, the addition of which she thought might give an added fillip to the dish. Then she decided to add a little onion paste ... and then a little sugar ... and so it went. Finally she steamed the fish in a pressure cooker and the result was something so delicious, different and mouth-watering that within minutes of being placed on the table the fish was all gone.

And so I added another recipe to my collection.

1 kg rui, cut in medium to small
pieces
250 gms green peas, shelled and
ground to a fine paste with a
little water
1 tablespoon turmeric paste
1 teaspoon chilli paste
2 cloves garlic, ground to a paste
1 inch piece ginger, ground to a
paste
1 onion, ground to a paste
4 tablespoons dahi
3–4 green chillies, slit
salt and sugar to taste
250 gms mustard oil

Place fish in *dekchi* or container in which you intend steaming.

Add all the other ingredients including oil and mix thoroughly.

Add salt and 1½ teaspoons sugar or to taste.

Cover container or *dekchi* with tight fitting lid or a piece of foil. Place in a large *dekchi* or pan.

Fill with hot water to come half way up to smaller container. Cover large *dekchi* with tight fitting lid.

Steam for half an hour or till fish is cooked.

Carefully remove small *dekchi* from the larger pan. Remove cover and pour fish into serving bowl.

At its best when not reheated.

In a pressure cooker at 15 lb pressure the fish should be cooked no more than 15 minutes.

Microwave method
In a suitable dish with lid (cling film can be used instead of a lid), mix together all the ingredients with the fish, including oil, salt and sugar. Place the mixture in the dish, cover and cook on high for 10 mins. Check to see if the fish is cooked, if not, cook on medium for another 5–7 mins or until done. Let stand covered for 5 mins. Serve.

A good accompaniment with: *Rice*

Serves: 8

6 thick pieces fish (rui, rawas, hilsa etc.) or any medium-sized whole fish

lump of ripe tamarind size of a golf ball or one tablespoon tamarind concentrate

½ cup of water

1 teaspoon sugar or to taste

½ teaspoon turmeric powder

2 green chillies, chopped

100 gms mustard oil

2 tablespoons mustard seeds, ground to a fine paste

½ teaspoon chilli powder

¼ teaspoon turmeric powder

6 green chillies, slit in half

2 teaspoons salt

In a bowl, mix together thoroughly the tamarind and water and then pass through a fine sieve into another bowl, discarding the rind and seeds. Add to the thickish juice half teaspoon turmeric, sugar, chopped chillies, one-third of the oil and part of the salt. Keep aside.

To mustard seed paste add the turmeric, chilli powder, salt, balance mustard oil and finally the green chillies.

First pour the tamarind pulp into a suitable sized oven-proof dish. Place the fish on top of tamarind pulp and then pour the mustard gravy mixture over the fish. DO NOT MIX.

Cover the top of the dish with close fitting lid or foil, and cook in a pre-heated medium-hot oven (350°F) for 25–30 minutes. This fish preparation has an unusual flavour—sweet-sour on one side and a mustardy flavour on the other. Should be served at table from the dish in which it has been cooked so that the colour—dark brown below and golden yellow on top—and the two flavours do not mix until served.

Hence the name *Ganga-Jamuna* which refers to the confluence of the two great rivers. Here, the two distinct colours—that of the darker Ganga and the lighter Jamuna—are clearly visible.

A good accompaniment with: *Rice*

Serves: 3–4

Muri Ghanto

Fish Head Curry cooked with Rice

½ kg fish head (rui, mrigel,
  katla, bekti or rawas)
1½ tablespoons cummin paste
1 tablespoon coriander paste
½ tablespoon turmeric paste
½ teaspoon chilli paste
1 tablespoon ginger paste
3 tablespoons uncooked rice,
  cleaned and washed
1 cup water (approx)
8–10 tablespoons oil
1 tablespoon ghee
4 bay leaves
½ tablespoon garam masala
  paste or powdered (see page 7)
salt to taste
1 teaspoon sugar

Wash fish head thoroughly and fry in hot oil until just browned. Remove from pan. With the wooden end of a knife or a mallet, break fish head into pieces.

In the same pan in which fish head is cooked add the *masala* paste to the remaining hot oil. Fry for about 5 minutes, then add the rice, mix thoroughly with the *masalas* and fry for about 5 minutes.

Add water and the broken fish head, salt and sugar to taste. Stir well.

Cover, reduce heat to a mild simmer and continue cooking, stirring from time to time, until nearly all the water is absorbed and rice is cooked.

In a separate pan, heat the ghee, add bay leaves, fry for a few minutes and then pour over *Muri Ghanto.*

Add *garam masala* pastes or powder to the *Ghanto.* Stir. Cook for a couple of minutes and remove from fire.

Small cubed potatoes may be fried and added to the *Muri Ghanto* towards the end of cooking period.

Variation:
Muri Ghanto can also be made with *mung* or *channa dal* instead of rice by substituting it for 250 gms *dal*, boiled and drained (must remain whole). Follow above recipe, adding the *dal* after the *masalas* are fried.

A good accompaniment with: *Rice*

Serves: 4–6

Asto Bekti Maacher Dom

Whole baked Bekti in Masala

1–1½ kg whole bekti fish
2 onions, halved and sliced fine
2 onions, ground to paste
1 tablespoon turmeric paste
1 teaspoon chilli paste
3–4 cloves garlic, ground to a
    paste
4–6 tablespoons dahi
4 tablespoons mustard oil or
    vegetable oil
garam masala (see page 7)
4 bay leaves
salt and sugar to taste
large piece foil to cover fish

Wash and clean the fish, removing the entrails but keeping the head intact. Make diagonal slashes on both sides of the fish. Rub half the garlic, ginger and onion pastes on the fish. Cover and put aside for half an hour.

Heat oil in a pan. Add sliced onion and fry to a golden brown.

Add *masala* paste balance to the pan and fry 5–7 minutes, sprinkling water as necessary. Ensure that *masalas* are well cooked.

Heat oven to 375°F or medium heat.

Place foil on large *thala* or flat dish. Place fish on the centre on the foil strip ensuring that there is sufficient foil on all sides to cover and seal the fish. Turn up sides of the foil.

Spoon half the prepared gravy over fish so that it is well coated with gravy. Turn the fish over in the foil and spoon the balance gravy over fish.

Bring ends of foil together and seal fish loosely in the foil. Place foil packet in centre of oven on baking sheet or heat-proof dish and bake 20–30 minutes or until the fish is cooked.

To serve, carefully remove fish to serving platter and spoon gravy over fish.

Note: Any other white flaky fish may be used instead of *bekti*.

A good accompaniment with: *Rice, Ghee Bhat*

Serves: 8

Baked Butter Bekti with Saffron Rice

1 whole bekti or other similar
    fish approx. 1½ kg–2 kg
500 gms. butter
2 onions*
6 cloves garlic*
1 large piece ginger*
1 cup parsley, chopped
salt and pepper
1 teaspoon flour

Saffron Rice:
2 cups cooked rice
500 gms green peas, cooked
100 gms butter
2 onions, chopped
½ teaspoon saffron mixed in
    1 tablespoon milk

*ground to a paste

Clean the fish, leaving both the tail and the head intact, and make 3 diagonal cuts across fish on both sides. Place the fish in a suitable dish and smear over with the onion-garlic-ginger paste. Marinate for several hours. (In India, keep in the refrigerator).

Half an hour before required for serving, heat oven to hot (400°F). Melt 500 gms butter. Place fish in a large dish suitable for baking and brush liberally with butter. Continue to cook fish on each side for approximately 15 minutes, brushing with butter from time to time. The fish should be cooked when it has turned a light brown and is flaky. Remove from oven and place on suitable serving platter. Keep warm.

Take the butter from the dish in which fish has been cooked, put in a small pan and heat thoroughly until butter bubbles. Stir in 1 teaspoon flour. Cook for a minute and then add the parsley, salt and pepper as required.

Place the Saffron Rice around the fish and pour butter sauce over all.

To make Saffron Rice
Heat the butter and fry the onions until transparent. Pour in cooked rice and cook at high heat for 10 minutes, stirring well and taking care that the rice does not stick to the bottom of the *dekchi*.

Add the cooked peas and cook a further 5 minutes.

Finally mix in the saffron and milk and fry for another 5 minutes.

Serve with fish.

Serves: 8–10

Parshé Maacher Jhal

Hot Curried Parshé Fish

6 medium-sized parshé/mullet
  (known in Bombay as boil)
1 large onion, halved and sliced
  finely
½ tablespoon turmeric paste
2 teaspoons chilli paste
4–6 green chillies, slit
a pinch onion seeds
4–5 tablespoons oil
½ cup water
salt to taste

In a large frying pan or *karai* heat the oil and lightly fry the fish. Remove from pan.

Reduce oil in pan to 3 tablespoons. Keep remainder for other use. Add the onion seeds to hot oil in pan and when spluttering stops, add the finely sliced onions.

Fry until onion changes colour and softens but before it can turn brown, add the turmeric and chilli pastes.

Fry the *masalas* well—about 5 minutes. Then add half cup water, green chillies and salt to taste. Let the gravy come to the boil.

Carefully lay the fish side by side in the pan and simmer over mild heat, spooning gravy over fish and shaking pan from time to time to ensure that fish does not stick to the bottom of the pan.

Remove from fire when only a very thick gravy remains.

Note: Any small fish can be substituted for *parshé.*

A good accompaniment with: *Rice*

Serves: 3–4

Koi

Climbing Perch

Koi is sometimes referred to as the *Climbing Fish*. It has come by this name because it has been known to climb on to branches of trees during floods by means of its very sharp fins. It is bred in tanks or lakes and is always purchased alive. Dead *koi* is considered something of a risk as it is known to carry germs. The size of a *koi* varies from approximately 4 to 6 inches. Being very bony, the larger sized *koi* is naturally in great demand. The killing and scaling of the fish is an art in itself. I would not recommend an amateur to try doing this without being taught. However, *koi* is a great delicacy with the Bengali and I have, therefore, included a recipe on *Koi*.

Tetul Elish and Sorse Elish Jhol

Chicken Korma and Dimer Curry

Bahu Khuda Ghee Bhat

Rui Macher Doi Mach and Rui Macher Ganga-Jamuna

Keema Curry

Fish Moulee

Chicken Malai Curry and Omelette Curry

Jhinge Chingri and Kumro Chingri

Koi Maacher Chorchori
Climbing Perch Curry

4 *large koi fish*
. 2 *tablespoons mustard paste*
1/4 *teaspoon turmeric paste*
1/4 *teaspoon chilli paste*
1/2 *onion, finely sliced*
1/4 *tsp whole mustard seeds*
4 *tablespoons mustard oil*
1/2 *cup water*

After killing and scaling fish, cut out gills from the side and remove entrails but do not remove head. With a knife make a couple of diagonal slashes on the body of the fish and coat lightly with quarter teaspoon turmeric and salt.

Mix together *masala* pastes with half cup water.

Heat oil in *karai* or pan and lightly fry the fish until the tails of the fish begin to curl. Remove and keep aside. Heat the remaining oil in *karai* and add the mustard seeds. When this stops spluttering, add the sliced onion. Fry until completely limp but not brown.

Through a strainer add the *masala* water and then salt to taste and the green chillies. Bring to the boil and then add fish.

Simmer gently until fish is done and oil comes to the surface leaving very little gravy in the pan.

A good accompaniment with: *Rice*

Serves: 2–4

Chittol Maacher Mondo

A special preparation with Feather Back Fish

In season, the *chittol* fish abounds in the rivers of East Bengal (Bangla Desh). It is a very tasty fish but it is also very bony. Therefore, only a certain portion of it is normally eaten. This delicious dish is made by the East Bengalis from those portions which are very bony and normally thrown away. The preparation is very time-consuming, but rewarding.

1 kg back of chittol in one piece, skin removed
2 medium-sized potatoes, boiled
salt
½ teaspoon black pepper, freshly ground
8 cups water
5–6 tablespoons mustard oil
2 tablespoons ghee
4 bay leaves
garam masala (see page 7)
2 onions ground to a paste
1 inch piece ginger, ground to a paste
2 cloves garlic, ground to a paste
1 tablespoon turmeric paste
1 teaspoon chilli paste

Holding the raw fish firmly at the end away from you, scrape fish towards you with a tablespoon.

The fish will come away in layers, leaving behind the bones.

When this task (and it is a task!) is completed, mix the fish with boiled potatoes, salt and freshly ground black pepper. Knead until the fish resembles dough.

Flatten to an oblong, an inch thick. Cut in 2-inch squares.

Have 8 cups water boiling in a large pan. Carefully drop fish cakes into the boiling water. Simmer 15 minutes or until cakes are spongy. Remove from boiling water with slotted spoon and cut each cake in four crosswise.

To make the curry:
Heat the mustard oil in a *karai* or pan and gently fry the fish cakes in oil. Remove when lightly browned. Drain oil and keep for other use.

In the same *karai*, heat the 2 tablespoons *ghee*. Add bay leaves and *garam masala*. Fry for 2 minutes. Now add all the other *masala* pastes and fry for 5 minutes, sprinkling water, if necessary, to prevent it catching at the bottom.

Add 2 cups water and let the gravy come to the boil. Add fish cakes and simmer gently until water is reduced to half.

Remove from fire.

A good accompaniment with: *Rice, Ghee Bhat*

Serves: 8

Elish Maach
Hilsa Fish

The hilsa is a sea-fish which comes into the estuary of the rivers of Bengal to spawn. Traditionally, we do not eat the hilsa after *Bijoya* or the end of the *Durga Puja* festival, until *Saraswati Puja*—a period of four to five and a half months. The tradition probably developed in order to allow the fish time to spawn. Coincidentally, the hilsa is not as flavourful from the months of October to February.

Species of the hilsa—the *bhing* and the *palla* are available in Bombay. I am told that the American river shad, however, is the nearest to the hilsa in flavour.

As the fish is normally sold whole, cutting and cleaning the fish properly yourself is important. Instructions given are those we follow in Bengal.

First remove scales from the fish.

Carefully cut the head of the hilsa from the body taking care that the bile bag does not burst or the fish will taste bitter when cooked. Depending on preference, the head can be cleaned and slit in half lengthwise and used in the preparation of a dish or it can be kept aside to be used in a *chorchori*.

Remove the entrails from the body of the fish and discard. If there is any roe, remove this also. Wash and cut it in pieces.

At this stage, wash the fish in water thoroughly. DO NOT WASH AGAIN.

Slice fish across in half-inch or three-quarters-inch thick pieces. A kilo or a kilo and a quarter of fish will give 10 to 12 pieces.

In order to obtain a larger number of pieces, first cut the fish vertically, keeping the spinal bone and a little more with the stomach end of the fish. Now cut the fish crosswise into half-inch or quarter-inch thick pieces. In this manner you get the triangular shaped, larger boned pieces with a hole in the centre called *peti* and the broader solid pieces from the bony back of the fish known as *gada*. It is important to keep the spinal bone with the *peti* otherwise these pieces may disintegrate while cooking.

Elish Bhaja

Fried Hilsa

6 pieces hilsa (palla or bhing)
1 teaspoon turmeric paste
salt
pepper or a little chilli powder if
    preferred (½ teaspoon)
oil for frying

Heat oil till blue haze appears.

In the meantime, coat the hilsa with turmeric paste and salt to taste.

Fry in hot oil until crisp and well browned.

Drain off oil and serve immediately.

Hilsa fried this way tastes best when the fish is really fresh and must be served immediately.

A good accompaniment with: *Rice* and *Dal* or *Khichuri*

Serves: 3–4

Elish Tetul

Fried Hilsa in Tamarind

The following recipe for hilsa is, as far as I know, an original of my great grandmother, Mrs.Man Mohan Ghose.

6–8 slices hilsa (pala or bhing)
2 balls tamarind, size of a golf
    ball or 2 tablespoons tamarind
    concentrate
1 cup water
1 teaspoon turmeric paste
sugar and salt to taste
3–4 tablespoons oil

In a bowl make a thick pulp with one cup water and tamarind. Discard the seeds and fibres of the tamarind after extracting juice. To tamarind pulp add the turmeric, salt and sugar and mix well. Coat the hilsa slices well with tamarind pulp.

In a pan heat oil till blue haze appears and carefully slide in the hilsa pieces one at a time, so that they cover the bottom of the pan but do not overlap. Pour in the remaining tamarind pulp. Continue cooking over high heat taking care that the hilsa does not stick to the bottom of the pan.

Carefully lift and turn the hilsa over once and continue to cook until the tamarind pulp is practically all absorbed and the oil can be seen on the surface.

Note: If your *karai* is small, fry a few pieces of hilsa at a time, and remove from pan. Finally add the remaining tamarind juice and cook down till oil appears on the surface. Add cooked hilsa and gently heat for 5 minutes.

A good accompaniment with: *Rice*

Serves: 4–6

Elisher Sorsé Jhol

Hilsa in Mustard Gravy

6–8 pieces hilsa
1 teaspoon turmeric paste
½–1 teaspoon chilli paste
  (optional)
4–6 teaspoons mustard paste
2–3 cups water
2 tablespoons oil
salt to taste
4–6 green chillies, slit

Heat oil in pan, and fry hilsa lightly for a few minutes.

In a bowl mix together turmeric, chilli paste, mustard paste with 2 cups water. Drain through sieve directly into the pan in which hilsa is cooking.

Add green chillies and salt to taste.

Reduce flame and continue cooking till fish is done. Plenty of gravy should remain.

The quantity of water to be used depends on how much gravy you prefer. If a very light gravy is wanted, add the extra cup of water.

A good accompaniment with: *Rice*

Serves: 4–6

Elish Maacher Kancha Jhol

Spiced Hilsa Stew

6–8 pieces hilsa
2 teaspoons turmeric paste
½ teaspoon chilli paste
⅛ teaspoon onion seeds
3 tablespoons oil
4–6 green chillies
1–1½ cups water

Heat oil in pan, and when quite hot add onion seeds. Fry a few minutes and then add hilsa, and continue frying for 2 or 3 minutes.

Mix the turmeric, chilli pastes and one cup of water. Pour this mixture directly into the pan in which the hilsa is cooking. Bring to the boil. Reduce heat so that mixture in pan continues to simmer.

Add salt to taste and green chillies and the dish is ready once the fish is cooked, the gravy thickens and oil comes to the surface.

A good accompaniment with: *Rice*

Serves: 4–6

Elish Maacher Tauk Jhol

Hilsa with Tamarind and Mustard

8–10 pieces hilsa—about 1 kg
1/2 teaspoon turmeric paste
1/2 teaspoon chilli paste
2 tablespoons mustard paste
1/4 tablespoon mustard seeds
4 tablespoons mustard oil
lump of tamarind, the size of a
    golf ball, or 1 tablespoon
    tamarind concentrate
3 cups water
salt to taste
1/2–1 teaspoon sugar
4–6 green chillies, slit

In a bowl, add 1 cup water and the tamarind, leave for 10 minutes and then slowly work with a spoon to extract all the juice from the tamarind. Throw away seeds and rind.

In a separate bowl mix the turmeric, chilli and mustard pastes in 2 cups water.

Heat the oil in a *karai* and when really hot, add mustard seeds. Cook till seeds stop spluttering. Add the pieces of hilsa very carefully.

Fry fish for a couple of minutes shaking the *karai* so that the fish does not stick to the bottom.

Through a sieve pour contents of the second bowl into the *karai* and then the tamarind juice. Bring it to a boil.

Add salt, green chillies and sugar.

Simmer 15 minutes.

There should be plenty of light gravy in this dish. Serve with plain boiled rice.

Variation
2–3 tablespoons vinegar may be substituted in place of tamarind.

Serves: 6

Elish Maacher Paturi

Hilsa with Mustard smoked in Banana Leaves

1 hilsa about 1–1¼ kg.
3 tablespoons mustard paste, very
  finely ground (preferably a mixture of the black and white
  varieties, ground with the
  addition of a green chilli to
  cut the bitterness).
1 teaspoon turmeric paste
1 teaspoon chilli paste
150–200 gms mustard oil
8–10 green chillies, washed and
  slit
6–8 banana leaves, halved.

Note:
1. Remeber the colour of the
   banana leaf will not change
   drastically.
2. For 1 kg of fish you would
   have to cook it in 2 batches,
   the time remains the same for
   each indivival batch.

Place cut pieces of fish in a medium-sized dish or aluminium *thala* and add the *masala* pastes and salt. Mix the fish and *masalas* together thoroughly, but carefully so as not to break the fish. Add the mustard oil and green chillies and mix again.

On a *tawa* or iron griddle, place 3 or 4 banana leaves one on top of the other and another 3 or 4 crosswise over the first ones. Carefully place the hilsa slices, well coated with *masala* in the centre of the banana leaves taking care to see they do not overlap. Pour all the oil and remaining *masala* gravy over it. Fold the banana leaves envelop fashion towards the centre from each side to make a 6 inch–8 inch square packet. Tie with a string.

Place *tawa* or griddle over very hot fire. The outer leaves will slowly burn through and the colour of the banana leaves will slowly change to a yellowish brown. The hilsa should be cooked within 20–25 minutes. Remove from *tawa*.

It is always better to cook this dish just before serving but it can be made ahead and rewarmed care- fully before serving.

To serve, place the banana leaf packet on a large platter. Carefully undo string, and open, tucking the over-hanging ends of the banana leaves under the platter.

Variation:
The fish is mixed with *masalas* and then placed in an over-proof dish to bake in a medium hot oven. Foil can replace banana leaves for on-the-stove cooking. The flavour naturally is different.

Microwave method
Follow the recipe as above, make indivival packets, or in a suitable dish place a banana leaf, place the pieces of fish on it so that they do not overlap, add the remaining *masala* and oil paste, cover with another banana leaf and tuck in to make a large packet. Cook on medium for 15 mins. Check to see if the fish is cooked then, if not cook for another 5 mins—let it stand for 5 mins covered—serve.

A good accompaniment with: *Rice*

Serves: 6

Doi Maach

Hilsa Fish in Yogurt

8–10 pieces hilsa
a pinch turmeric powder
   (1/8 teaspoon)
a small piece ginger, coarsely
   chopped
1/2 teaspoon salt
500 gms dahi
3 tablespoons ginger paste
1 teaspoon salt
1 tablespoon ghee
1–2 teaspoons sugar
1/2 teaspoon onion seeds
8–12 green chillies, slit

Sprinkle the turmeric powder and half teaspoon salt over hilsa. Coat evenly. Place in a small bowl, add the pieces of ginger. Cover bowl with foil and place in a large pan. Fill pan with hot water to come three-quarters of the way of the side of the bowl. Put pan on fire and steam fish for 20 minutes.

In the meantime beat *dahi* lightly with fork. Add ginger paste, 6 green chillies, sugar and salt. Mix together gently.

When fish is cooked, remove the sliced ginger and pour the fish, including whatever gravy has accumulated in the bowl, into *dahi* mixture. Coat the fish thoroughly with the *dahi* mixture and cover with tight lid.

In a pan heat the *ghee* to smoking, add the onion seeds and cook until seeds stop spluttering. Add remaining green chillies, cook another 2 minutes and then pour the *ghee* over the fish in *dahi*. Mix well.

Arrange fish coated with *dahi* on a serving plate and pour remaining gravy over it. Cover. After 3 or 4 hours fish is ready for serving.

Preferably served cold or at room temperature.

Note: Other fish such as mackerel may be substituted. If filleted fish is used see that the fillets are not more than half-inch thick.

A good accompaniment with: *Rice*

Serves: 6

Narkel Chingri Bharta

Prawn Bharta in Coconut

250 gms prawns or shrimps
1 whole semi-ripe coconut
2 tablespoons mustard paste or
   prepared mustard
2 green chillies, chopped fine
1/2 onion, minced fine
salt to taste
2–4 tablespoons mustard oil
a little stiff flour dough
a piece of foil sufficiently large to
   completely seal coconut

If prawns are used, peel, clean and chop. If shrimps are large treat in a like manner.

Pierce 3 holes in the coconut at the end where 3 markings can be seen. Drain off water.

In a bowl mix together the chopped prawns, mustard paste, chillies, onion and oil. Add salt to taste.

Stuff the prawn mixture into the coconut through the 3 holes. When coconut is quite full (all the prawn mixture should be used), plug the holes with flour dough. Cover coconut completely with foil to seal and press foil with hands to shape on to coconut.

Bake coconut in a hot oven for 2 hours after which remove foil and crack coconut in half. The meat of the coconut should have loosened from the shell and the fish and coconut should come out as two large chunks.

Mash with fork, and if too dry, add a little more mustard oil.

Add salt to taste and serve.

The original recipe calls for the coconut to be covered in clay and then baked in dying coals. For convenience foil has been substituted and the coconut is baked in an oven.

A good accompaniment with: *Rice*

Serves: 2–4

Chingri Cutlets

Prawn Cutlets

8 *large fresh prawns*
1 small onion, ground
*1 small piece ginger, ground to a
    fine paste*
2 cloves garlic
½ lime juice
1 egg
1 tablespoon flour
1 cup toasted bread crumbs
oil for frying

Chop off the heads of the prawns. Peel off shells keeping tails intact. Make an incision down the back of prawn and remove black entrail. Now, with a sharp knife cut prawn practically in half down the back. Flatten out the 2 halves with a mallet or the flat end of a broad knife. Beat prawn to a one-eighth-inch thickness.

Shape by rounding off the upper portion of the prawn, i.e., the portion away from the tail and taper it down towards the tail to look something like an elongated balloon. Shape all the 8 prawns in this way.

Place prawns in a flat dish and coat with the onion, garlic and ginger pastes and the lime juice. Sprinkle with a little salt. Let the prawns marinate for several hours, turning them over once or twice.

About 15 minutes before you serve the prawn cutlets, break the egg into a basin. Add the flour and whip gently to blend.

Add a little salt to the egg mixture.

Spread bread crumbs over a large piece of wax paper.

Take the prawns one at a time. Dip in the egg, coating well.

Then coat with bread crumbs.

After coating with crumbs, pat the prawns into shape again, dusting off excess crumbs.

Heat oil in a frying pan till smoking and fry prawns to a golden brown colour.

Serve with french fried potatoes and a salad.

Note: May be deep-fried but caution must be taken to keep shape of cutlets.

This is an Anglo-Indian recipe but for convenience has been placed in this section.

A good accompaniment with: *Salad* and *potato chips*

Serves: 4

Chingri Cutlet Curry (1)

Prawn Cutlet Curry

8 large fresh prawns, to be
   prepared and cooked as
   directed under Chingri Cutlets
2 tablespoons oil
2 onions, sliced
1 tablespoon turmeric paste
2 teaspoons chilli paste
1 teaspoon garam masala paste
   (see page 7)
3 cups water
2 teaspoons ghee
garam masala (see page 7)
3 or 4 bay leaves
salt and sugar to taste

The prawn cutlets should be prepared a little in advance and allowed to cool.

Heat oil till smoking, add the onions and fry till soft and golden brown.

Add turmeric and chilli pastes and fry for about 5 minutes.

Add the water. Sprinkle salt and a quarter teaspoon sugar.

Stir.

Cook for about 10 minutes.

Add the garam masala paste and then carefully slip in the cutlets so that they do not overlap or touch each other. With a spoon keep pouring the gravy on the prawn cutlets allowing them to gently simmer in the curry sauce for about 15 minutes.

In a separate pan heat the 2 teaspoons ghee, add the bay leaves and the garam masala, cook until they stop spluttering and pour over the prawn cutlet curry.

Carefully turn the cutlets over. Holding pan on two sides, shake pan over the fire two or three times and remove from heat.

To serve, first carefully remove cutlets and place in serving dish and then pour gravy over.

A good accompaniment with: Rice or Luchi

Serves: 4

Chingri Cutlet Curry (2)

Prawn Cutlet Curry

This delightful recipe is another from the vast collection of late Mrs.C.R.Das. 8 large prawns prepared as directed under *Chingri Cutlet* crumbed and fried (see general instructions).

1 coconut grated and 2 cups coconut milk obtained
6–8 green chillies, chopped fine
1 teaspoon salt
2 limes, juice extracted
1 tablespoon cummin seed, fried and ground to powder
sugar to taste

Half an hour before serving, place a large *dekchi* on the fire with the coconut milk. Let it come to the boil and simmer over a brisk flame.

Add salt, sugar and chopped green chillies to the coconut milk.

When the milk is thickened and creamy, slip in the fried prawn cutlets.

Simmer for approximately 10 minutes.

Remove from fire and sprinkle lime juice over curry.

Then carefully remove cutlets to serving dish and pour gravy over.

Finally sprinkle with cummin powder and serve.

A good accompaniment with: *Rice, Ghee Bhat, Luchi*

Serves: 4

Chingri Maacher Kabiraji Cutlet

Prawn Cutlet with Egg Batter

8 *large prawns*
8 *small prawns (optional)*
¼ teaspoon turmeric powdered
¼ teaspoon chilli powder
1 large onion, chopped
*4-inch piece ginger**
*3 cloves garlic**
1 teaspoon black pepper, freshly
  powdered
6 eggs
2 tablespoons besan (chick-pea
  flour)
1 tablespoon water
1 onion, halved and sliced fine
2–3 green chillies, chopped fine
salt and pepper to taste
oil for deep frying

*ground to paste

Prepare the large prawns as for Prawn Cutlets but continue to flatten until paper thin.

Prepare the smaller prawns like the larger ones. But with the tails removed. Place over large flattened prawns and beat into the large prawns, thus forming very thin but large cutlets. Mix the powdered turmeric and chilli with the ground *masala* paste and coat the cutlets on both sides with this mixture. Sprinkle the powdered pepper and half teaspoon salt over both sides of the cutlets and marinate for a couple of hours.

Prepare the batter by whisking the eggs well and then adding the 2 tablespoons *besan* and finally 1 tablespoon of water until mixture is frothy.

Mix in the chopped onion, chillies and then half teaspoon of salt and a pinch of pepper.

Heat oil in a frying pan, and when smoking put in one prawn cutlet at a time well coated with batter.

Using a tablespoon add an additional tablespoon of batter (including some of the chopped onions and chillies) over the cutlet as it fries. Turn and fry the other side also pouring over additional batter.

Remove when batter turns a golden colour.

Note: As large prawns are difficult to get now, Prawn Cutlets, the Cutlet Curries and the *Kabiraji Cutlet* can all be made with small prawns or shrimps. There will be some extra work involved in shaping the cutlets and it may be necessary to use a little fresh bread with the shrimps or prawns in order to bind them together.

Serve with a salad made of thin sticks of cucumber, beetroot and onion with a lime squeezed over it.

A good accompaniment with: *Any salad, tomato sauce*

Serves: 8

Chingri-Alu-Phulkopir Dalna
Prawns with Potatoes and Cauliflower

250 gms small prawns
1 medium-sized cauliflower
250 gms medium-sized potatoes
1 onion, sliced fine
4 bay leaves
garam masala (see page 7)
1 onion, ground to a paste
1 tablespoon turmeric paste
1 teaspoon chilli paste
1 teaspoon ginger paste
1 tablespoon coriander paste
½ teaspoon cummin paste
½ teaspoon garlic paste
1 teaspoon sugar
salt to taste
6–8 tablespoons oil

Remove heads from prawns. Peel and shell, but keep tails intact. Make an incision down the back and remove black entrail. Wash prawns, dry and rub with a little salt and about half teaspoon turmeric. Keep aside.

Cut cauliflower into medium-sized flowerets, wash, drain and keep aside.

Peel potatoes and quarter. Wash, drain and keep aside.

Heat oil to smoking in *karai* or pan.

Lightly fry the prawns for 2–3 minutes, drain and keep aside. Now fry the cauliflower and potatoes in the same pan until just turning brown. Drain and keep aside with prawns.

Measure oil in pan. Remove all but 2–3 tablespoons. Bring to smoking hot and add bay leaves and *garam masala*. Fry a couple of minutes and then add sliced onions. Stir-fry onions until just turning brown. Now add all the ground *masala* pastes and the ground onion. Stir-fry sprinkling with water as necessary until *masalas* change colour and are cooked.

Add potatoes and cauliflower to *masalas* mixing well. Reduce heat, cover and cook for 5–10 minutes. Check from time to time that the *masalas* are not catching at bottom of pan. If very dry add ½–1 cup water. Mix well and simmer until potatoes and cauliflowers are cooked. Add the prawns, adjust seasoning adding sugar at this time. Simmer 5–7 minutes longer and remove from fire. There should just be very little gravy in the pan.

Substitute frozen shrimps if prawns are not available. In which case, cut the cauliflower and potatoes smaller.

Add the shrimps without frying. Cook as above.

A good accompaniment with: *Rice* or *Luchi*

Serves: 4

Choto Chingrir Chorchori

Shrimps with Vegetables

1 cup cleaned, shelled shrimps
4 potatoes, halved lengthwise and
cut across in 1/8-inch thick
slices
2 large onions halved lengthwise
and then sliced fine
1/2 tablespoon turmeric paste
1 teaspoon chilli paste
4 green chillies, slit
4 green peppers (capsicum) in 1
inch long strips (optional)
2 tablespoons oil
a pinch of onion seeds

Heat oil in pan, and when smoking hot, add the onion seed. Fry for a couple of minutes and then add the sliced potatoes. Stir and fry until potatoes begin to change colour.

Add sliced onions, the turmeric and chilli pastes. Stir well and fry for several more minutes (5–7 minutes).

Now add half cup water to the contents of the pan and allow to simmer, stirring from time to time. Add the green chillies and salt to taste.

When the water is completely absorbed, and the potatoes nearly cooked, add the shrimps. Stir and fry until shrimps are done.

Now add the capsicum strips and cook for approximately 7 minutes more or until green peppers are quite limp.

Alternative directions for cooking:
Cook as above until the point where onions are added to the potato with the turmeric paste. Mix well, cover pan and cook over reduced heat for 5–7 minutes. Add green chillies, salt and shrimps and continue cooking over medium flame until potatoes are nearly done. Add sliced green peppers, stir in with potatoes and shrimps, cover pan and cook for 2 minutes. Remove cover and stir-fry until green peppers are limp and potatoes are cooked. Remove from fire.

I personally prefer the second method of cooking.

A good accompaniment with: *Rice* or *Luchi*

Serves: 4

Chingri Dhoka Dom

Steamed Prawn Cakes Curried with Yogurt

To make Dhoka—Prawn cakes:
*500 gms prawns or shrimps
    cleaned and shelled
1 tablespoon channa dal (chick-
    peas)
2 green chillies
½ teaspoon peppercorns*
4-inch piece ginger*
2 cloves garlic*
2 teaspoons green coriander
    leaves, chopped
1 teaspoon powdered
garam masala (see page 7)
2 tablespoons ghee
1 coconut, grated
2 onions, halved and finely sliced
12-inch length of foil
oil for frying dhoka (approx
    150 gms)*

ground to a paste

For the curry:
*½ tablespoon turmeric paste
1 teaspoon chilli paste
2 onions, ground to a paste
1 teaspoon garlic paste
1 tablespoon ginger paste
½ cup dahi
2 bay leaves
garam masala (see page 7)
2 cups water
3 tablespoons ghee
salt and sugar to taste*

Soak the *dal* overnight in water. Chop the prawns, and grind together into a thick paste with grated coconut and the soaked *dal*. Mix in the ground *masala* paste.

Heat the *ghee* in a pan and brown onions till just turning crisp. Add the *ghee*, coriander leaves, *garam masala* and salt to the prawn paste. Mix well. The paste should be semi-solid.

Place the paste in a dish approximately one inch deep or on the centre of the piece of foil and pat into an oblong approximately half-inch thick. Fold foil over to completely seal in the prawn paste.

In a suitable sized pan, heat water until simmering and carefully immerse the foil packet with prawn paste into the water. Cover pan and steam prawn gently for 30–40 minutes.

The prawn paste can be placed in a pressure cooker pan and steamed for 15 minutes under 15 lb pressure instead of steaming in a pan.

Remove packet from water and when cool enough to touch, open foil packet and cut the shrimp paste (which should now be quite solid), diagonally into diamond shapes or into squares.

Heat oil in *karai* and fry the *dhoka* until lightly browned. Remove when done and drain off oil.

Heat *ghee* in a pan till smoking and then add the bay leaves and *garam masala*.

Fry for a couple of minutes. Add the ground *masala* paste and onions. Fry the *masala* for several minutes sprinkling with water as necessary so that it does not catch at the bottom of the pan.

When *masala* is well fried add half cup of the remaining water, and the prawn cakes, salt and sugar as preferred. Bring to a gentle simmer and cook 10 minutes.

Mix the *dahi* and the remaining water together and strain into pan.

Simmer for another 10–12 minutes and remove from fire.

Sandesh

Jal Khabar

Chingri Malai Curry

Rabeyas Prawn and Bamboo Shoot Curry

Chingri Maacher Paturi and Chingri Maacher Chorhori

Jhinge Posto

Bonde, Darbesh, Rasogolla, Pantua and Chanar Jilipi

Parshe Maacher Jhol

Variation:
The prawn *dhoka* can be cooked as for *Malai* Curry using thick coconut milk instead of *dahi*.

A good accompaniment with: Rice, Luchi or Ghee Bhat

Serves: 6

Chingri Maacher Paturi

Prawns cooked in Banana Leaves

1 kg prawns, cleaned, shelled and heads removed
4 tablespoons mustard paste
1 teaspoon turmeric paste
½ teaspoon chilli paste
100 gms mustard oil or a little more if liked
6–8 green chillies
salt to taste
8 banana leaves
a few toothpicks

Place the banana leaves cross-wise alternatively on an iron *tawa* or griddle.

Mix together thoroughly the prawns and the next five ingredients. Add salt to taste and mix again.

Pour prawn mixture carefully into centre of banana leaves. Fold leaves over towards centre and pin together to form a packet.

Place *tawa* over very high heat. The heat will slowly discolour the outer layers of banana leaves and at the same time cook the prawns. After 15 minutes, take the *tawa* off the fire, undo the packet and with a spoon carefully turn prawns over. Seal the packet with a toothpicks again, replace on *tawa* over hot fire and cook yet another 10–15 minutes.

Remove the banana leaf packet on to a platter, undo and carefully tuck the overhanging ends of the leaf under and serve.

The banana leaf can be substituted by foil. And the dish can be baked in a medium hot oven.

Large-sized frozen shrimps may be substituted for prawns. Care should be taken to completely defrost the shrimps and squeeze out any excess moisture.

Microwave method
Mix prawn and all other ingredients and make a packet as above. Place in a suitable container. Cook on medium for 8 mins. Undo the packet, stir prawns in, cover and cook on medium for another 8 mins. Let it stand for 5 mins. Serve on the banana leaf

Note: Banana leaf will not change colour like in the conventional method of cooling

A good accompaniment with: Rice

Serves: 6–8

Chingri Bhaté or Bhapé

Steamed Prawns

*1 kg prawns, cleaned and
   chopped into bite-size piece*
4 tablespoons mustard paste
½ tablespoon turmeric paste
½ teaspoon chilli paste
6–8 slit green chillies
salt to taste
*2 medium onions, halved and fine-
   ly sliced*
6 to 8 banana leaves
string

Mix the prawn as for *paturi* but include onions. Pack into banana leaves also as for *paturi* but tie well with the string and make absolutely certain that the packet is completely sealed.

The orthodox method of cooking this dish is to carefully drop the packet into the rice while it is boiling and it cooks at the same time as the rice. Remove the packet with a slotted spoon before draining rice. Cooking by this method is called *bhaté (Bhat* = rice, *bhaté* = cooked in rice).

Place the packet in a suitable pan without any handle, but a close fitting lid.

Place this inside another pan, 2 or 3 times as large. Pour hot water into the larger pan to come one-third up the side of the smaller pan.

Place on fire and simmer for 30 minutes (replenishing the hot water as required to keep it at the same level). Remove from heat.

Remove the pan containing banana packet from the water. Take out the packet, untie and serve as for *paturi*.

Microwave method
Mix all the above ingredients together with the prawns. Place the mixture in a suitable dish with a lid (cling film can be used instead of a lid). Cook on high power for 5 mins, remove cover/lid, stir well, replace cover and cook for another 6–8 mins, or till the onions are soft. Let it stand covered for 5 mins. Serve.

Notes: Banana leaves can be used to make a packet as described in *Chingri Paturi* (page 124).

The prawns may also be steamed without the banana leaf covering. In this case, of course, the flavour will be somewhat different.

Steaming can also be done in a pressure cooker in which case a lot of time is saved.

Substitute: Frozen shrimps.

A good accompaniment with: *Rice*

Serves: 8

Chingri Daab

Prawns cooked in Green Coconut Shell (Daab)

1 kg prawns
250 gms onion
6–12 green chillies, slit
1 grated coconut
4 tablespoons mustard seed paste
1 teaspoon powdered turmeric
1½ teaspoons salt
4–6 tablespoons mustard oil
1 daab, cut half-inch from top
    horizontally and water removed

Preparation of Daab

Take a green coconut (daab), cut flat an inch from bottom for coconut to stand upright. From top end, cut 1–½ inch and make an aperture on the top surface of the nut, large enough for tablespoon to enter. Remove water, retain top with stalk as lid.

Shell, clean and remove heads from fresh prawns. Chop into small pieces.

Slice the onions in half and then slice lengthwise very fine.

In a bowl mix all the ingredients, finally adding oil and then mix thoroughly.

Stuff the *daab* with this mixture and use the top half-inch slice as a lid. Seal with a piece of foil to cover the top of the *daab*.

Bake in a 350°F oven for approximately one hour in which time the prawns should be cooked and the mustard oil should have risen to the top of the shell.

This dish is best when served in the *daab* shell and makes a glamorous addition to a buffet table.

Microwave method

Mix prawns and all other ingredients together. Stuff *daab*. Add 1½ teaspoons oil on top, cover with *daab* lid. Place in microwave and cook on medium power for 25–30 mins. Let it stand for 5 mins. Serve from the *daab*.

Substitute: Fresh or frozen shrimps.

A good accompaniment with: *Rice*

Serves: 6–8

Choto Chingri Kofta

Shrimp Balls

500 gms shrimps, shelled and
    cleaned
60 gms ginger, very finely
    chopped and shredded
1 onion or a bunch spring onions,
    finely chopped (part of the
    leafy tops of the green onions
    may be used)
2 eggs
1½–2 tablespoons flour
2 green chillies finely chopped,
    seeds removed
2 cloves garlic, minced fine or
    ground to paste
1 teaspoon salt
½ teaspoon black pepper, freshly
    grated
oil for deep frying

In a bowl mix together all the above ingredients to a rather stiff batter.

Heat oil till smoking and drop batter in small round balls into oil. Cook to a golden brown.

Substitute: Frozen shrimps

Variation:
Boneless fish, finely flaked may be used instead of prawn.

Serve with tomato ketchup. Delightful as a cocktail snack.

Serves: 6–8

Choto Chingri Kofta Curry (1)

Curried Shrimp Balls

For Kofta:
500 gms shelled shrimps, chopped
1 tablespoon ginger, finely minced
2 cloves garlic, finely minced
2 green chillies, finely minced
  (seeds removed)
¼ teaspoon turmeric powder
4 tablespoons besan (chick-pea
  flour)
4–6 tablespoons water
1½ teaspoons salt
1 teaspoon black pepper, freshly
  grated

For Curry Sauce:
1 coconut grated and 2 cups thin
  milk and 1 cup thick milk
  extracted (see general instruc-
  tions)
¼ teaspoon turmeric paste
2 tablespoons ginger paste
½ teaspoon garlic paste
salt
1 teaspoon sugar
8–10 green chillies, slit (optional)
1 tablespoon ghee
3–4 bay leaves
garam masala (see page 7)
juice of 1 lime

Mix all the ingredients for the *kofta* together in a bowl, adding sufficient water to make a semi-solid batter and set aside.

In a large *dekchi*, bring to the boil the thin coconut milk and add to this the turmeric, ginger and garlic pastes, salt and half teaspoon sugar, also the slit green chillies. Boil for about 10 minutes, then turn down heat to gentle simmer.

Drop medium-sized balls of the shrimp batter into the simmering coconut milk, taking care that the balls do not touch until shrimp balls have cooked in the coconut milk at least 10 minutes.

Add the thick coconut milk, stir and cook for a further 10 minutes.

Heat the tablespoon *ghee* with bay leaves and *garam masala* and pour this over the *kofta* curry. Stir and remove from fire.

Finally add juice of one lime.

Substitute: Frozen shrimp

Variation:
Boneless fish, finely flaked, may be substituted for shrimps.

A good accompaniment with: *Rice* or *Ghee Bhat*

Serves: 4–6

Choto Chingri Kofta Curry (2)

Curried Prawn Balls

Prepare *koftas* from 500 gms of shrimp as directed in shrimp *koftas* but make larger balls using approximately 1 tablespoon of the batter for each ball. Now prepare the curry sauce with the following ingredients:

2 tablespoons oil
1 onion, sliced
1 onion, ground to paste
1 tablespoon turmeric paste
1 teaspoon chilli paste
1 coconut grated; 1 cup thick milk and 1 cup thin milk extracted (see general instructions)
salt to taste
1 teaspoon sugar
1 teaspoon garam masala paste (see page 7)
1 teaspoon ghee
2 bay leaves
garam masala (see page 7)
1 tablespoon fresh coriander leaves (optional), chopped
6 green chillies slit

Heat oil to smoking.

Add onion and fry to golden brown but while still limp add the ground onion and other *masala* pastes.

Fry for 7–10 minutes, stirring all the time, and then add 1 cup thin coconut milk. Add salt and sugar, stir and let it simmer until coconut milk is reduced to half or less.

Drop the fried *koftas* into the *dekchi*, with the green chillies. Bring to the boil.

Pour in the thick coconut milk and continue to simmer.

Do not place lid over *dekchi*.

Remove from fire when gravy has thickened.

Heat the *ghee*. Fry bay leaves and *garam masala* for a couple of minutes and pour over the *kofta* curry. Adjust seasoning.

Sprinkle with green coriander leaves.

Substitute: Frozen shrimps

Variation:
Use fish koftas

A good accompaniment with: *Any cereal*

Serves: 4–6

Chingri Malai
Prawn Coconut Curry

500 gms prawns, shelled and
   cleaned
2 medium onions, sliced fine
2 onions, ground to a paste
3 teaspoons ground turmeric paste
1 teaspoon chilli paste
2 bay leaves
garam masala (see page 7)
2 tablespoons ghee
salt to taste
1 teaspoon sugar
1 coconut from which 1 cup thin
   milk and 1 cup thick milk is
   extracted (see general instructions)

Warm *ghee* in pan, and when very hot add bay leaves and *garam masala* and fry for a few minutes.

Add sliced onions and fry to golden brown.

Then add ground onions and the next two ingredients and continue frying until *masalas* are well fried but does not stick to the pan.

Add the prawns and stir thoroughly with the *masalas* and cook for just a few minutes before adding the 1 cup thin coconut milk. Add sugar and salt to taste. Simmer over brisk flame until the gravy is less than half.

Then add the 1 cup thick coconut milk and cook another 10 minutes when the curry is ready.

Variation:
A small amount of ginger and garlic paste may be added.

Substitutes:
Preferably frozen prawns. If not available, the large-sized frozen shrimps.

A good accompaniment with: *Rice, Ghee Bhat* or *Luchi*

Serves: 4–6

Rabeya's Prawn and Bamboo Shoot Curry

I got this particular recipe from my cousin Rabeya who makes the most delightful Prawn and Bamboo Shoot Curry I have ever tasted.

1 kg prawns, shelled and washed
1 bamboo shoot
1½ coconuts, grated from which
   1 cup thick and another
   2 cups thin milk have been
   extracted (see general instructions)
2 large or 4 medium onions
   ground to a paste
½ teaspoon garlic paste
1 tablespoon ginger paste
1 teaspoon turmeric paste
1 teaspoon chilli paste
4 tablespoons oil or ghee
salt to taste
1 teaspoon sugar

Peel bamboo shoot, and then slice into thin rounds, and finally into julienne strips.

Soak in salted water overnight.

In the morning drain. Wash thoroughly. Boil in fresh water to cover. Drain.

Heat oil in pan and lightly fry the prawns and remove from pan. Now add the ground onion paste and then the other *masala* pastes and fry over a hot flame for about 5 minutes.

Add the prepared bamboo shoot; mix thoroughly.

Add the thin coconut milk and simmer over high flame until liquid in pan is reduced to half. Add prawns. Mix thoroughly with the gravy.

When nearly dry, add 1 cup thick coconut milk.

Continue cooking until only a very thick gravy remains in pan.

Substitute:
Fresh or frozen shrimps. Tinned bamboo shoot may be used after washing thoroughly.

Note: Bamboo Shoots are now available preserved in salt. Apart from being soaked over night in cold water, it needs to be boiled twice with a change of fresh water each time. As it is preserved with salt, after cooking check to see if you need to add any salt.

A good accompaniment with: *Rice* or *Luchi*

Serves: 8

Chingri Vindaloo

Prawn Vindaloo

1 kg cleaned prawns
1 tablespoon turmeric paste
2 teaspoons chilli paste
1 teaspoon coriander paste
1 teaspoon cummin paste
2 teaspoons ginger paste
½ teaspoon garlic paste
1 tablespoon mustard paste
salt to taste
2 teaspoons sugar or to taste
3–4 tablespoons vinegar
100 gms mustard oil
2–3 cups water

Heat oil in deep heavy pan. Add the next seven ingredients after prawns. Fry for several minutes.

Add vinegar and the prawns. Keep frying until all the vinegar is absorbed.

Add water and let it come to the boil.

Add salt and sugar.

Simmer for 20 minutes or until the water is reduced by about a quarter and the prawns are cooked. Remove from heat.

Reheat before serving.

Substitute:
Fresh or frozen shrimp.

A good accompaniment with: *Rice*

Serves: 6–8

Galda Chingri Bhaja

Fried Freshwater Crayfish or Lobster

4 galda chingris or crayfish
2 onions, halved and sliced fine
½ green pepper (capsicum), seeds
    removed and sliced in julienne
    strips
1 teaspoon black pepper, freshly
    powdered
¼ teaspoon turmeric powder
¼ teaspoon chilli powder
¼ teaspoon garlic, paste or finely
    minced
1 teaspoon ginger, paste or finely
    minced
salt to taste
2 tablespoons oil
2 teaspoons flour with a little
    water to form sticky paste
4 eggs*
2 tablespoons flour*
2 tablespoons water*
¼ teaspoon salt*
ghee or oil for frying crayfish

*Blended together in a bowl

Cut the crayfish in half through the shell, using a pair of scissors. See that the head and tail of the fish remain in one piece. Cut right through flesh of the fish and divide in 2. Remove the black intestinal sack. Cut the flesh of the crayfish into bite size pieces.

Reserve coral if any.

Heat *ghee* in a pan. Add the sliced onion and fry till opaque. Add the green pepper and fry 5–7 minutes. Add the chopped crayfish and coral. Stir-fry a couple of minutes.

Add the powdered *masalas*, the garlic and ginger. Stir-fry until crayfish is cooked and the *masalas* blended in about 10–12 minutes. Remove from fire.

Stuff the halved crayfish shell with the cooked crayfish. Stuff head of crayfish also. Place 2 halves together and seal with a thick flour paste. Spoon the blended egg-flour-water batter over the fish. See that it is well coated. Heat *ghee* in a large fry pan. Fry the crayfish until the egg batter is set and lightly browned and the shells have turned a pinky-red. Turn once, or roll while frying and add more batter, if necessary, to completely cover fish.

A good accompaniment with: *Salad*

Serves: 4

Galda Chingri Curry

Curried Crayfish or Lobster

4 medium sized crayfish
   (approx 1 kg)
4 potatoes, quartered
2 onions, ground to paste
1½ tablespoons turmeric paste
2 teaspoons chilli paste
1 teaspoon ginger paste
1 teaspoon garlic paste
1 coconut grated and a cup thick
   milk and 1 cup thin milk
   extracted (see general
   instructions)
2 bay leaves
garam masala (see page 7)
oil for frying crayfish and potatoes
2 tablespoons ghee
salt to taste
1 teaspoon sugar

Clean crayfish. Remove shell from body of fish, but do not discard shell over head. Smear with half tablespoon turmeric paste and a sprinkling of salt. Fry fish until it changes colour. Keep aside.

In the same pan, lightly brown the potatoes and keep aside. In a *karai* or pan heat *ghee*. Add bay leaves and *garam masala*. Fry a couple of minutes and then add the onion and other *masala* pastes. Stir and cook until *masalas* change colour.

Add sugar and salt to taste. Stir-fry sprinkling with water until *masalas* are well cooked.

Add the thin coconut milk. Cover *karai* and bring to the boil. Add crayfish and potatoes. Simmer over a brisk fire until potatoes are cooked. Stir *karai* from time to time.

Add the thick coconut milk. Simmer over a brisk flame for 10 minutes, then remove from fire.

A good accompaniment with: *Rice*

Serves: 4

Kakkrar Chorchori

Dry Curried Crab

4–6 medium-sized raw crabs
1¼ tablespoons turmeric paste
2 teaspoons chilli paste
1 tablespoon ginger paste
4 onions, halved and sliced fine
a pinch panch phoran
2 tablespoons oil
salt to taste
1 cup water

Clean the crabs, scrubbing them well.

Remove the hard shell of the crab and discard. Cut away the spongy inedible portion on the under side of the crab. Cut the claws from the body and crack. Cut the crabs in half if preferred.

Coat the crab and claws with quarter tablespoon turmeric paste and a sprinkling of salt. Fry in oil till claws and crab are lightly browned. Keep aside.

To the oil in the same pan, add the *panch phoran* and when spluttering stops, add sliced onion and fry until just brown, then add all the *masala* pastes. Stir and fry 5 minutes.

Return crabs and claws to pan. Stir in with *masalas*. Add salt.

Add 1 cup water. Bring to the boil and cook until there is practically no gravy in the pan.

Note: Crabs are always bought alive. Cooked crabs may be used, but the taste will change.

A good accompaniment with: *Rice*

Serves: 8–10

Kakkrar Curry

Crab Curry

4 large raw crabs
4 potatoes, quartered
2 onions, ground to a paste
2 onions, halved and sliced fine
1½ tablespoons turmeric paste
2 teaspoons chilli paste
1 tablespoon ginger paste
½ teaspoon garlic paste
2 bay leaves
garam masala (see page 7)
oil for frying crabs and potatoes
2 tablespoons ghee
salt and sugar to taste
2 cups water

Scrub crabs clean. Separate claws from body and crack. Remove hard shell of crab. Rub in a little turmeric and salt and fry until lightly browned. Keep aside.

In the same pan fry the quartered potatoes only until lightly browned. Keep aside.

In a *karai* or pan, heat 2 tablespoons *ghee*. Add bay leaves and *garam masala*. Stir-fry a couple of minutes. Add sliced onions and stir-fry till brown.

Add all the *masala* pastes, salt and sugar to taste, stir and cook until *masalas* change colour, sprinkling with water as necessary.

Add 2 cups water, the fried potatoes and crabs. Cover and simmer gently until potatoes are done. Sugar may be added at the same time as the water.

A good accompaniment with: *Rice*

Serves: 4–6

Kethor Jhol

Turtle Curry

Please do not kill turtles
Today they are an endangered species.
    When this book was originally written, there was no ban on the consumption of turtle meat. We have retained the recipe as in our culture the turtle was considered a delicacy.

500 gms turtle meat
1 tablespoon black pepper paste
2 tablespoons coriander paste
1 tablespoon cummin paste
½ tablespoon turmeric paste
1 tablespoon garlic paste
2 tablespoons ginger paste
3 tablespoons mustard oil
1 tablespoon ghee
2 bay leaves
garam masala (see page 7)
salt and sugar to taste

Heat the oil till smoking hot. Add the turtle meat and fry for 5 minutes.

Add all the *masala* pastes and stir-fry another 10–15 minutes or until turtle meat and *masalas* are well blended and fried.

Add 4 cups water. Stir. Cover and simmer over medium heat until turtle meat is cooked.

In a fry pan or *karai*, heat *ghee*. Add the bay leaves and *garam masala* and when spluttering stops, pour over the *Kethor Jhol*. Stir and simmer a few minutes, then remove from fire.

Note: 4 medium potatoes quartered may be added.

A good accompaniment with: *Rice*

Serves: 4–6

MANGSHO, MURGI O DIM

MEAT, CHICKEN AND EGGS

Mangsho, Murgi O Dim
Meat, Chicken & Eggs

It is only in comparatively recent years that meat and chicken preparations have found a place in the Bengali cuisine. Even today, Bengalis prefer the meat of the young goat, *patha* and in our markets, castrated goat, *khassi* sells at a premium over sheep meat (mutton) which the Bengali considers as having too strong a flavour.

Except for *Pathar Jhol*, most of the other recipes in this section appear to be adaptations from those of the North. However, even today, the larger part of meat cooking in Bengal must be attributed to the Muslim influence. The Moghul conquest of India and the spread of Islam throughout the country had its effects in Bengal too. Ruled by Muslim Nawabs over centuries and a large meat-eating Muslim population, Bengali cuisine adapted itself to include the meat dishes introduced by the Muslims. Many of the recipes in this book are very typically *Bengali Muslim* in character.

However, except in the affluent households where a meat preparation is normally served at dinner, a meat or chicken dish is prepared only for special occasions. The Bengali seldom eats pork or other meat.

Tomato Chutney, Aamer Chutney, and Anaras Chutney

Mangsho O Lal Kumro and Mangshor Ghugni

Chanar Kalia

Jhal Freizee

Daab Chingri

Alu Dam

Poached Eggs in Tomato Gravy

Alu Chops

Pathar Jhol

Spiced Mutton Stew

500 gm very fresh, young goat
    meat cut into cubes
1 sliced onion
1 tablespoon black pepper, freshly
    ground
1½ tablespoons cummin paste
1 tablespoon coriander paste
4 tablespoons mustard oil or any
    other oil
2 teaspoons ghee
3–4 bay leaves
a few green chillies, slit
6 cups water
salt to taste
½ teaspoon sugar

Heat mustard oil until blue haze appears, then add goat meat cut in chunks and *masala* pastes and fry briskly for 10–15 minutes. Add water and when this comes to the boil, add the salt and sugar.

Cover and simmer over a medium fire until meat is cooked (about an hour).

In a separate *dekchi* or pan, heat the *ghee*, add bay leaves, green chillies and sliced onions.

Fry until onions are just brown, then pour in some of the gravy from the meat. Mix well and then pour back into the *dekchi* containing the *Pathar Jhol*.

Place *dekchi* over a brisk fire, bring to the boil.

Remove from fire.

A good accompaniment with: *Boiled Rice*

Serves: 4–5

Mangshor Curry (1)

Mutton Curry

400 gms mutton, cut in 1½ inch
  cubes
4–6 potatoes, peeled and quartered
2 onions, halved and sliced fine
2 onions, ground to a paste
1½ tablespoons turmeric paste
1 teaspoon chilli paste
1½ teaspoons ginger paste
½ teaspoon garlic paste
salt and sugar to taste
6 tablespoons ghee or oil
water as required

Heat *ghee* till blue haze appears. Fry sliced onions to a golden brown.

Add the onion, chilli, turmeric, ginger and garlic pastes.

Fry for five minutes.

Add cubed mutton.

Add salt. Mix well. Cover and cook 7–10 minutes.

Remove cover from pan and stir-fry until all natural juices of the meat are absorbed.

Add water to cover. Reduce flame. Cover and simmer for at least an hour.

Remove cover. Check the meat which should be more than half done.

Add quartered potatoes and sugar as preferred. Cover and simmer gently for another half an hour.

The curry should be ready to serve.

Variations:

1. Add a couple of chopped tomatoes to the fried *masala* pastes. Fry until *ghee* comes to the surface. Then continue as above.

2. The number of potatoes to be added depends on the number of persons eating. With the addition of four potatoes, the above measure will give four large helpings. With six potatoes added, the meat cut a little smaller, the curry will stretch to feed six.

A good accompaniment with: *Rice, Luchi* or *Porota*

Serves: 4–6

Mangshor Curry (2)

Mutton Curry

*500 gms mutton cut into 1½ inch
  cubes*
4 onions, 2 sliced very fine
2 onions, ground to paste
1½ tablespoons turmeric paste
1½ teaspoons chilli paste
1 tablespoon ginger paste
*2 large cloves garlic, ground to a
  paste*
1 tea cup dahi
salt to taste (approx 1½ teaspoons)
a pinch of sugar
4 tablespoons ghee
water as required

In a bowl mix together with the mutton, all the *masala* pastes, *dahi*, onion paste, salt and sugar. Cover and leave for an hour.

In a *dekchi* or pan, heat *ghee* and fry the sliced onions until just brown.

Add the mutton and salt, mix well. Cover and cook for about 7 minutes. Remove cover from pan and continue cooking for about 10–15 minutes or until meat juices are absorbed, stirring all the time so that the meat or *masalas* do not catch at the bottom of the *dekchi*.

Add water to cover. Bring to the boil.

Cover and simmer over a low heat for another 1 hour 15 minutes, approximately.

Remove from fire when meat is cooked.

A good accompaniment with: *Rice, Luchi* or *Porota*

Serves: 4–5

Mutton Curry (A quick preparation)

500 gms mutton, cut into 1½
    inch cubes
4 medium-sized onions, halved
    and sliced fine
1 level teaspoon powdered turmeric
½ teaspoon chilli powder or more
    if desired
½ inch piece ginger, shredded or
    chopped very fine
2 cloves garlic, chopped very fine
4 medium potatoes, cut into fours
salt to taste
a pinch of sugar
2 tablespoons oil or ghee
4 cups water

Heat *ghee* in a *dekchi.*

Fry onions to a golden brown.

Add the meat and salt to taste, mix and fry for 5 minutes.

Then add all the *masalas* and continue stirring and frying for another 10–15 minutes on a slow flame or until there is no gravy.

Add the water, cover *dekchi* and simmer over medium heat for about an hour, when meat should be nearly done.

Add the potatoes and continue simmering until the meat is tender and the potatoes are cooked.

To pressure cook this curry, heat *ghee* in pressure cooker and cook as directed above, until all the natural juices of the meat are dry.

Add 2 cups water and pressure cook under 15 lb pressure for 15 minutes.

Cool pressure cooker, remove lid and add potatoes. Close lid of the pressure cooker; bring under pressure and pressure cook another 3 minutes.

Remove cooker from fire. Cool. Remove lid and serve.

A good accompaniment with: *Rice, Luchi* or *Porota*

Serves: 6

Mangshor Kofta Curry

Meat Ball Curry

For the Kofta:
½ kg minced mutton (fat free)
1 slice white bread, soaked in a
   little milk
1 onion, minced fine
1 tablespoon ginger paste
½ teaspoon garlic paste
2 green chillies, chopped very fine
1 tablespoon green coriander
   leaves, chopped fine
1 teaspoon garam masala powder
   (see page 7)
½ teaspoon salt

For the Curry:
4 potatoes, quartered
1 tablespoon turmeric paste
1 teaspoon chilli paste
1 tablespoon ginger paste
2 onions, ground to a paste
1 onion, sliced fine
salt and sugar to taste
8–10 tablespoons ghee or oil

To make the Koftas/Meat Balls:
Wash the mince well and remove any membrane present.
Grind to a very fine paste with a mortar and pestle or in a food processor.
Squeeze milk from bread and then add the bread to the ground mince and mix well.
Add the ginger and garlic pastes, the green chillies and the coriander leaves.
Finally add salt and the powdered *garam masala*. Mix thoroughly.
Knead the mince for a few minutes with the hands as you would dough. Divide mince into 12 to 16 equal portions and form into balls.
Heat the *ghee* in a pan and fry the mince balls of till a golden brown. Remove from pan and keep aside.

To make the Curry:
In the same pan, in the remaining *ghee*, fry the potatoes and when just turning brown, remove from pan and set aside.
Remove all the *ghee* leaving only 2 tablespoons in the pan.
When very hot, fry the sliced onion until brown.
Add the onion paste, the turmeric, chilli and ginger pastes.
Fry for 5–7 minutes, sprinkling water, if necessary.
When the *masalas* are well fried, add salt and a little sugar to taste. Add two cups hot water and bring gravy to the boil. Boil for 5 minutes.
Add the potatoes, and after about 10 minutes, add the fried *koftas*. Simmer over medium heat only until potatoes are done and the gravy is reduced to half.
Remove from fire.

A good accompaniment with: *Ghee Bhat, Plain Rice, Luchi* or *Porota*

Serves: 4

Mangshor Gota Moshla

Mutton Curry cooked with Whole Spices

1 kg mutton
250 gms dahi
200 gms ghee
8–10 whole dry Kashmiri chillies
8–10 cloves
12–15 peppercorns
500 gms onions, halved and
    finely sliced
150 gms ginger, finely sliced
150 gms garlic, finely sliced
½ teaspoon saffron / kesar
1 tablespoon milk
salt to taste

Cut the mutton into large pieces. Add sliced onion, garlic and ginger, *dahi* and *ghee*. Mix thoroughly. Add the whole spices and Kashmiri chillies, mix again and marinate for an hour.

The conventional method of cooking this dish is to seal the *dekchi* with some flour paste. Place over a very slow fire and during the last 45 minutes of cooking, place burning charcoals on the lid of the *dekchi*. This takes about 2½–3 hours to cook.

I improvise by sealing the *dekchi* with a piece of household foil, cutting this slightly larger than the lid, and then placing it over the lid and crimping in the edge to seal. I use an oven pre-heated to 300°F, and cook for 2 hours. Increase the heat to 350°F for the last half an hour of cooking. The result is practically the same but cooking becomes much simpler.

Remove *dekchi* from heat after 2½ hours cooking. Mix saffron in 1 tablespoon milk and then mix this into the curry. The saffron should melt in the hot curry and give it a lovely colour and flavour. Can be made early in the day and heated just before serving.

Note: No water is added at any time when cooking this dish. It is essential, therefore, to seal the *dekchi* as thoroughly as possible so that no steam escapes. It is also essential that the meat should be cooked over a very slow fire. Care should be taken to see that the *masalas* at the botton of the *dekchi* do not burn or stick, so you may require to shake the *dekchi* from time to time. If cooking in an oven, this becomes unnecessary.

To pressure cook:
Combine all the ingredients together, add 2 teaspoons *besan* (chick-pea flour). Mix well.
    Cook under 15 lb pressure for half an hour.
    DO NOT ADD ANY WATER

Variation:
Similar to *Gota Moshla* is a *Mutton Razala*, a speciality Muslim recipe. The ginger and onion in this case are ground to a paste. The rest of the recipe is as above.

Add: 1 teaspoon sugar. Breast meat is preferred.

Note: If the mutton or lamb is fatty, then no oil or cooking medium is required.

A good accompaniment with: *Porota* or *Plain Rice*

Serves: 6–8

Mangshor Dopiaza

Mutton and Onion Curry

500 gms mutton, cut in cubes
500 gms onion; 250 gms halved
   and sliced fine, 250 gms
   halved and cut into thick slices
1 tablespoon cummin paste
2 teaspoons chilli paste or to taste
½ teaspoon onion seeds, roasted
   and powdered (optional)
1 cup dahi
3 or 4 bay leaves
1 teaspoon black pepper, freshly
   ground
1 tablespoon ginger paste
1 teaspoon garlic paste
6 green cardamoms, powdered
½ teaspoon powdered garam
   masala (see page 7)
½ cup ghee (approx)
1 cup water
salt to taste

Heat the *ghee* till smoking.

Add the finely sliced onions and fry until a golden brown.

Using a slotted spoon, drain onions and keep aside.

Reheat *ghee* to smoking hot and add the mutton, fry until well browned.

Remove mutton from *dekchi*.

Reheat *ghee* and add the cardamom powder, chilli, pepper and cummin paste. Fry for a couple of minutes and add the *dahi*, thickly sliced onions and the browned meat.

Stir and after cooking for about another 15 minutes, add salt to taste, the fried onions and three-quarter cup water. Simmer over very low heat until meat is tender.

Add the garlic and ginger paste to the remaining quarter cup water and pour over the meat. Sprinkle the onion seed powder over the meat. Stir and continue to cook over a very low fire until only a very thick gravy remains.

Sprinkle *garam masala* over meat before serving.

Variation:
I sometimes add 4 medium tomatoes quartered, at the same time as the *dahi* and thickly sliced onions.

A good accompaniment with: *Porota*, *Luchi* or *Ghee Bhat*

Serves: 4–5

Husseini Curry

Mutton Kabab Curry

500 gms lean boneless mutton
250 gms small pearl onions
3 or 4 large pieces of ginger
16–20 stiff broomsticks or bamboo
    or metal skewers
    approx 6 inches long
4 tablespoons ghee or oil
4 tablespoons dahi
1½ tablespoons turmeric paste
1 tablespoon chilli paste
4 bay leaves
garam masala (see page 7)
1 onion, chopped
salt and sugar to taste

2 cloves
2 cardamom
2 inch cinnamon

Boil the mutton in one piece until three-quarters done.

Drain stock from mutton and keep aside for use later.

Cut the mutton into 1-inch cubes.

In the meantime, peel the onions, and keep ready.

Peel the ginger and slice into very thin rounds.

Scrape broomsticks until smooth.

Skewer ginger, boiled mutton, onion in this order until the skewer is quite full, ending with a slice of ginger.

Now heat oil in pan. Add the bay leaves and *garam masala*.

Stir-fry for a couple of minutes.

Add chopped onion and brown.

Add the turmeric and chilli paste and fry for about 5 minutes.

Add the *dahi* whipped lightly.

Mix well with the *masalas*, adding salt to taste.

Add 1½ cups mutton stock and simmer for about 7–10 minutes.

Add the prepared skewers and simmer gently until onions and meat are quite cooked and there is a thickish gravy in the pan.

To serve, place skewers side by side in a large serving dish and pour the gravy over.

Note: Husseini curry can be made from leftover roast.

A good accompaniment with: *Ghee Bhat* or *Luchi*

Serves: 4–5

Kabab

500 gms lean mutton
1 tablespoon coriander seed*
2-inch piece of ginger*
2 cloves garlic*
2 inch piece green papaya*
1 teaspoon poppy seed*
8 tablespoons dahi
1 teaspoon chilli powder
a pinch turmeric powder
salt to taste
metal skewers to grill kababs

*ground to a smooth paste

Cut mutton into 1½-inch cubes. Mix with ground paste, *dahi*, chilli and turmeric powder. Place in a cool place to marinate for several hours or overnight, mixing two or three times.

Just before *kababs* are cooked, add salt to taste and mix well.

Skewer mutton on metal skewers and grill over a charcoal fire till well browned and cooked. An electric or gas grill may be used instead of a charcoal fire.

Note: If green papaya is not available, a commercial meat tenderiser may be used (e.g. papain extract).

A good accompaniment with: *Porota*

Serves: 4

Mangshor Ghugni (1)

Mutton with Green Peas

1 kg green peas, shelled
150 gms mutton (lean meat), cut
   in small cubes
¼ teaspoon chilli powder
2 teaspoons garam masala powdered (see page 7)
2 teaspoons cummin, roasted and
   powdered
2 teaspoons pepper, freshly
   ground
2 onions, ground to a paste
1 onion, halved and sliced fine
125 gms potatoes, peeled and
   diced into ½ inch cubes
1 coconut, diced small
2-inch piece ginger, peeled and
   finely shredded
125 gms ghee (about ½ cup)
4 bay leaves
3–4 whole dry red chillies
3 cups water (approx)
salt and sugar to taste

Heat about 50 gms of the *ghee* and to this add the green peas.

Fry until colour changes.

Add approximately 1½ cups water, a teaspoon each of powdered *garam masala*, pepper and cummin.

Continue cooking until peas become soft and near-ly all the water is absorbed.

While peas are cooking, in a separate *karai* add all but 1 tablespoon of *ghee*.

Fry the diced potatoes until lightly browned. Remove and keep aside.

Then fry the coconut until just turning brown and keep this aside with potatoes.

In the remaining hot *ghee*, fry the sliced onion till brown.

Add meat, mix well.

Add the onion paste and the chilli powder.

Fry for 5 minutes after which add the balance pow-dered *masala*.

Continue stirring and frying meat, sprinkling water, if necessary, for another 10 minutes or so.

Then add the balance of the 1½ cups water and simmer meat over medium flame until cooked and nearly all the water is absorbed.

If the pans in which the peas and meat have been cooked are not large enough to take the two together, use a larger pan and mix together the green peas and cooked meat.

Add to this the fried potatoes and coconut.

In a separate *karai* or pan, heat the remaining 1 tablespoon *ghee*, add the bay leaves and whole red chillies, cook for a few minutes and pour over the *ghugni*.

Mix well.

Set the *ghugni* over a medium fire, add salt, sim-mer for about 5 minutes.

Remove from fire.

A good accompaniment with: *Radhaballobhi Luchi* or *Luchi*

Serves: 10–12

Mangshor Ghugni (2)

Mutton with Chick-peas

250 gms Kabuli channa/chick-
    peas/whole Bengal gram
125 gms mutton, diced into ¼
    inch cubes
100 gms ghee/oil (about ½ cup)
2 onions, halved and sliced
60 gms. ginger, shredded fine
2 teaspoons cummin seeds,
    roasted and powdered
2 teaspoons black pepper, freshly
    ground
2 teaspoons freshly powdered
    garam masala (see page 7)
½–1 teaspoon chilli powder
4 whole red chillies
125 gms potatoes, peeled and
    diced into ¼ inch cubes
1 coconut (diced into small pieces)
3 cups water
2 teaspoons sugar
salt to taste

Prepare chick-peas by soaking in water for 5–6 hours or over-night and cook as directed under *Ghugni* (page 29)

Heat about 60 gms *ghee* in a *karai* and fry the chick-peas for about 10 minutes.

Add half the powdered *masalas* and shredded ginger.

Mix well.

Add 2 cups water.

Add salt to taste.

Continue cooking over brisk fire until chick-peas are done, and nearly all the water absorbed.

In another pan add all but 1 teaspoon of the *ghee*. Heat. First fry the diced potatoes and keep aside. Then fry the coconut and keep aside.

Add sliced onions to the hot *ghee* and fry until just turning brown.

Add the meat and continue braising the meat, stirring all the time.

Add the chilli powder, remaining powdered *masala* and ginger.

Fry well for another 10–15 minutes sprinkling water as required so that the *masalas* do not catch at the bottom of the pan.

Finally add the remaining water, salt to taste and continue to simmer over a medium heat until mutton is cooked and the water nearly all absorbed.

Add the potatoes and the coconut to the meat about 10 minutes before taking meat off the fire.

In a large pan heat the remaining *ghee*.

Add bay leaves and whole red chillies. When chillies stop spluttering, pour in the chick-peas and then the cooked meat. Stir.

Adjust seasoning.

Serve hot.

A good accompaniment with: *Radhaballobhi Luchi* or *Luchi*

Serves 4–6

Manghsho O Lal Kumro

Mutton and Red Pumpkin Curry

500 gms mutton, cut in small
  cubes
500 gms red pumpkin, skinned
  and sliced fine
1 onion, ground to a paste
1½ teaspoon ginger paste
½ teaspoon garlic paste
2 teaspoons turmeric paste
1 teaspoon chilli paste
2 tablespoons cummin paste
4 tablespoons ghee
2 bay leaves
garam masala (see page 7)
1 onion halved and sliced fine
salt to taste

Heat 3 tablespoons *ghee* in a pan till smoking hot.

Add the pieces of mutton and fry until lightly browned.

Add the *masala* pastes and fry.

Continue frying until all the natural juices from the meat is absorbed.

Add the sliced red pumpkin.

Add salt to taste (approx 1½ teaspoons).

Mix well. Reduce flame to medium. Cover and simmer 10–15 minutes without removing cover.

Remove cover. Stir. The pumpkin should have given out quite an amount of water and the meat should cook in this.

Continue to simmer meat and pumpkin over a mild heat. Stir from time to time so that it does not catch at the bottom of the pan.

Add half cup water at a time, if necessary.

When the meat is cooked there should be very little gravy in the pan.

In a separate pan heat the remaining tablespoon of *ghee*.

Add *garam masala* and bay leaves and fry till spluttering stops. Add sliced onion and fry till crispy brown.

Pour the *ghee, garam masala* and fried onions on to the Mutton Pumpkin Curry. Stir well. Simmer another 5 minutes.

Remove from fire.

A good accompaniment with: *Luchi* or *Plain Rice*

Serves: 6

Mangshor-Capsicum-Piaj Curry

Mutton, Green Pepper and Onion Curry

500 gms mutton, cut into 1½
    inch chunks
250 gms capsicum (green pepper)
    halved with seeds and white
    stringy portion removed and
    cut into pieces, the same size
    as meat.
250 gms small whole onions
    (pearl onions) peeled
6 tablespoons ghee or vanaspati
2 onions, chopped fine
1 tablespoon turmeric paste
1 teaspoon chilli paste
2 onions, ground to a paste
1 tablespoon ginger paste
1 teaspoon garlic paste
¼ teaspoon of onion seeds
4 cups water
salt to taste

Heat *ghee* and add the onion seeds. Immediately as this stops spluttering, add the chopped onion and fry till just brown, then stir in all the *masala* and onion pastes and fry for another 5–7 minutes.

Add the meat and salt to taste. Mix well and continue frying for 12–15 minutes, stirring all the time.

Add the water, cover *dekchi* and simmer meat for 45 minutes.

Remove cover.

Add the small whole onions, stir in with meat.

Cover and continue cooking for another half an hour. Then remove cover from pan.

Add the capsicums, mix well, cover again and cook for about 10–12 minutes or until capsicums are just done.

Meat should by now be quite tender and pearl onions well cooked. Remove from fire.

A good accompaniment with: *Luchi, Porota* or *Rice*

Serves: 6

Murgi Curry

Chicken Curry

1 medium-sized chicken
    (approx. 750 gms), cut in pieces
4 potatoes, peeled and quartered
2 tomatoes, chopped or quartered
2 onions, halved and sliced fine
2 onions, ground to a paste
1½ tablespoons turmeric
2 tablespoons chilli paste
1 tablespoon ginger paste
1 teaspoon garlic paste
salt and sugar to taste
4 tablespoons ghee

Heat *ghee* in pan. Fry the sliced onions till well browned but soft. Add the onion paste together with all the *masala* pastes. Stir-fry for 5 minutes or until *masalas* change colour. Add the tomatoes and stir-fry a few minutes more.

Add the chicken, stir-fry another 7–10 minutes. Sprinkle with a little water, if necessary. Add salt and sugar to taste.

Add 4 cups water, stir, cover and simmer chicken over medium heat until three-quarters done (approximately 45 minutes to an hour), stirring from time to time.

Add the quartered potatoes. Stir and cover pan. Cook till potatoes and chicken are both done and gravy has thickened.

A good accompaniment with: *Rice, Ghee Bhat* or *Luchi*

Serves: 4

Murgi Malai
Chicken in Coconut Gravy

1 medium chicken (approx 750 gms), cut in small pieces
1 coconut grated to make 1 cup thick and 2 cups thin milk extracted (see general instructions)
½ tablespoon turmeric paste
2 teaspoons chilli paste
1 tablespoon garlic paste
2 onions, halved and sliced fine
6–8 green chillies, slit
salt and sugar to taste
3 tablespoons ghee
4 bay leaves

Heat the *ghee* in a *dekchi* or pan. Add the bay leaves and fry a couple of minutes. Then add the sliced onions and fry till lightly browned.

Add the *masala* pastes and stir-fry five minutes and then add the pieces of chicken. Stir and cook until the natural juices of the chicken are all absorbed.

Add 2 cups thin coconut milk, the green chillies, salt and sugar, if preferred, and simmer over a medium brisk flame until chicken is done.

Add thick coconut milk and continue cooking over brisk flame for another 7–10 minutes and then remove from fire.

A good accompaniment with: *Rice* or *Ghee Bhat*

Serves: 4

Murgi Korma
Chicken in Yogurt

1 medium-sized chicken (approx 750 gms), cut in large pieces
2 onions, halved and finely sliced
2 onions, ground to a paste
1 tablespoon turmeric paste
2 teaspoons chilli paste
1 tablespoon ginger paste
1 teaspoon garlic paste (optional)
salt and sugar to taste
6 tablespoons dahi
4–5 tablespoons ghee
4 bay leaves
garam masala(see page 7)

Heat 4 tablespoons *ghee* in a *dekchi* or pan. Add the sliced onion and fry till brown but still soft.

Add chicken pieces and stir-fry until lightly browned.

Add all the *masala* pastes including onions, salt and sugar to taste and stir-fry several minutes sprinkling with water if necessary.

Blend the *dahi* in with 2 cups water. Add to the chicken.

Stir. Reduce heat, cover and simmer gently until chicken is soft and cooked.

In a separate pan, heat 1 tablespoon *ghee*. Stir-fry the bay leaves and *garam masala* until spluttering stops. Pour over *Murgi Korma*.

Stir and remove from fire.

A good accompaniment with: *Porota* or *Luchi*

Serves: 4

Murgi Gota Moshla

Chicken cooked with Whole Spices

1 medium chicken (approx 750
   gms), cut in medium sized
   pieces
5–6 medium-sized onions, halved
   and sliced fine
100 gms. ghee
150 gms dahi
6 large Kashmiri chillies
4 bay leaves
10 cloves
12–15 whole peppercorns
60 gms ginger, finely sliced
60 gms garlic, finely sliced
   (optional)
200 gms. or 3/4 cup dahi
1½ teaspoons salt or to taste
a pinch saffron soaked in a
   tablespoon of milk

Mix together in a *dekchi* all the ingredients except saffron. Leave to marinate for half an hour, turning from time to time.

When ready for cooking, cover *dekchi* with tight fitting lid and cover lid with a piece of foil so as to completely seal *dekchi*.

Place over a *very slow* fire and cook for 2 hours.

Remove from fire. Remove foil and uncover *dekchi*. Stir chicken and test if done. Cover with lid and seal again with foil.

Place in a preheated 275°F–300°F oven and cook for another half an hour till chicken is tender (it may also be cooked over a very low flame).

Remove from oven. Uncover *dekchi* and stir the saffron soaked in milk into chicken the curry. Cover *dekchi* and leave till time to serve.

Reheat gently before serving.

Note: If the chicken is fatty, the quantity of *ghee* should be reduced. The proportion given above is for skinned chicken.

A good accompaniment with: *Rice* or *Luchi*

Serves: 4

Murgi and Bansher Korol

Chicken and Bamboo Shoot Curry

1 bamboo shoot
1 chicken (approx 1 kg), cut in
    small pieces
4 onions, ground to paste
1 teaspoon garlic paste
1 tablespoon ginger paste
1½ teaspoons chilli paste
1 teaspoon turmeric paste
5 tablespoons oil or ghee
salt to taste
1 grated coconut to make 1 cup
    thick milk and 2 cups thin
    milk (as per general instruc-
    tions)

Peel bamboo shoot, slice into thin rounds and then into julienne strips. Soak in salted water overnight. In the morning drain and wash the bamboo shoot thoroughly.

Boil in fresh water until soft. Drain.

Heat oil in pan and lightly fry chicken pieces.

Remove from pan. Now add ground onion paste to oil in pan, stir and add the other *masalas*. Then add two cups thin coconut milk.

Reduce heat and simmer the chicken until nearly done.

Add the bamboo shoot and continue cooking, stirring continually, until the coconut milk is completely absorbed.

Now add 1 cup thick coconut milk, mix thoroughly with *masalas* and chicken in pan.

Simmer until only a very thick gravy remains in pan.

Note:
1 medium-size tin bamboo shoot can be used. Drain, rinse well and drain again, then cut into julienne strips. Add when chicken is nearly done.

Bamboo shoot preserved in salt is now available. Apart from soaking in cold water overnight, you need to boil it thrice, replenishing with fresh water each time. Also add salt only after cooking.

A good accompaniment with: *Rice*

Serves: 8

Dimer Bharta

Mashed Boiled Eggs

4 eggs, hard boiled and shelled
½ onion, grated or minced fine
1 green chilli, chopped very fine,
    with seeds removed (optional)
2 tablespoons mustard oil
salt to taste

Mash the eggs very fine.

Add all other ingredients and salt to taste. Mix well.

Divide into 4 or 6 portions.

Form into balls and serve.

Variations
1. Butter may be used instead of mustard oil.
2. Add a piece of mango from any *achar* chopped very fine.
3. Reduce the number of eggs to 2 and add instead 2 large well boiled and mashed potatoes.

A good accompaniment with: *Rice* and *Dal*

Serves: 4

Dimer Bora

Small Egg Fritters

4 eggs
½ onion, minced fine
¼ teaspoon black pepper, freshly
    powdered
¼ teaspoon cummin seeds pow-
    dered
1 green chilli minced fine, seeds
    removed
2 tablespoons besan (chick-pea
    flour)
salt to taste
ghee for frying boras (fritters)

Whip the eggs. Add all the other ingredients and whip until fluffy.

Heat *ghee* in a fry pan. Add a tablespoon (or 2 tablespoons if you want larger pancakes) of the batter to the pan.

Fry for 2 minutes or until batter has solidified. Flip over and fry the other side.

Remove when golden brown.

Variation:
Dimer Mamlet

As above, but omit besan. Eggs are only lightly whipped. Divide in 2 portions and fry as two large flat omelettes.

A curry can be made with *Dimer Mamlet*. The recipe for curry would be similar to that of Omlette Curry.

A good accompaniment with: *Rice* and *Dal* or *as a snack*

Serves 5–6

Dimer Curry

Egg Curry

4 large chicken or duck eggs
4 potatoes, peeled and
    quartered
1 onion, halved and sliced
    fine
1 onion, ground to a paste
½ tablespoon turmeric paste
½ teaspoon chilli paste
1 teaspoon ginger paste
¼ teaspoon garlic paste
    (about 2 cloves)
4 tablespoons ghee or
    vegetable oil
garam masala (see page 7)
salt and sugar to taste
2 bay leaves
2 tomatoes, chopped

Hard boil the eggs. Shell. Make 3 or 4 vertical slashes on the white of the eggs.

Heat *ghee* in *karai* or pan. Fry the eggs light brown, remove and keep aside.

In the same pan, brown the quartered potatoes and keep aside.

Keep only 2 tablespoons of *ghee* in *karai* (the balance, if any, can be put to other use). Fry the bay leaves and *garam masala* until spluttering stops.

Add sliced onions and fry till golden brown, but soft.

Add the turmeric, chilli, ginger and garlic pastes. Fry for 5–7 minutes, sprinkling water as necessary to keep the *masala* from burning.

Add chopped tomatoes and keep frying until oil comes to the surface.

Add two cups water, salt and sugar to taste. Let the gravy come to the boil. Add fried potatoes and eggs.

Reduce heat and simmer until gravy thickens and the potatoes are quite cooked.

Remove from fire.

A good accompaniment with: *Rice* or *Porota*

Serves: 2

Omelette Curry

4 eggs
½ onion, minced fine
1 green chilli slit, seeds rem-
    oved and chopped very fine
ghee for frying omlettes
2 tablespoons ghee for curry
1 onion, halved and sliced fine
½ tablespoon turmeric paste
½ teaspoon chilli paste
1 teaspoon ginger paste
¼ teaspoon garlic paste
2 tomatoes, chopped fine
garam masala (see page 7)
2 bay leaves
salt and sugar to taste

Prepare 2 omelettes using 4 eggs adding filling with minced onions and chillies. Cut each omlette into 3 to 4 pieces.

In a *karai* or pan heat 2 tablespoons *ghee*. Fry *garam masala* and bay leaves until spluttering stops.

Add sliced onions and fry to a golden brown.

Add all the *masala* pastes and fry for 5–7 minutes, sprinkling with water as necessary to stop *masalas* from burning.

Add chopped tomatoes and continue frying till oil comes to the surface.

Add 2 cups water and bring gravy to the boil.

Reduce heat to mild simmer after 5 minutes and slip in the omlette pieces.

Simmer until gravy is reduced to nearly half. The omelettes should remain intact.

A good accompaniment with: *Rice*

Serves 4

ANGLO-INDIAN RECIPES

Anglo-Indian Dishes of Bengal

There are certain dishes introduced into the Bengali cuisine by the Anglo-Indian Community of Bengal. Into this category fall such dishes as *Mince Curry, Pork Vindaloo, Potato Chops, Cutlets, Pantaras* and *Tomato Farci*. Except, perhaps, for *Egg Curry* and *Bora*, the egg dishes included in this book may also be said to be Anglo-Indian in character.

The influence of English, French, Portugese and Dutch colonists have all contributed to the variety of Anglo-Indian cooking, while of course, the British Raj played a major part.

The names *Pantaras, Tomato Farci, Fish Coorkit*, etc. are obviously corruptions from the French Chef's culinary vocabulary. I cannot remember a cook that my mother employed whose repertoire did not include *Potato Chops* (*Alu Chops*, they called it), *Pantaras* and *Tomato Farci*. These dishes and several others similar to them, were generally referred to as the *side dish* and served before the main course of the meal.

Alu-Chop

Potato Chops with Mince Filling

8–10 large potatoes, boiled and
   mashed
mince filling as for Pantaras (see
   page 166)
2 eggs*
1 tablespoon flour*
browned bread crumbs
ghee for frying chops

*mixed together

Divide mashed potatoes into 8 or 10 equal portions. Shape each portion into a cup and fill half with mince. Carefully close top of potato cup by pressing together. Form into flattened egg-shaped chops.

Coat in egg-flour batter and then coat in crumb. Dust off excess crumbs.

Heat *ghee* in fry pan and fry till brown. Drain off *ghee* and serve.

Potato Chops are a popular addition to a Bengali marriage feast and are usually made one-third the size given above.

Variation:
Fish, mixed vegetables, green jackfruit or *chhana* (*panir*) filling can be substituted.

A good accompaniment with: *Any salad, tomato sauce*

Serves 4–6

Meat Croquettes

500 gms minced meat
2 tablespoons ghee
2 onions, minced fine
1 teaspoon ginger paste or
*   shredded ginger*
¼ teaspoon powdered garam
*   masala (see page 7)*
4 slices fresh bread, soaked in a
*   little milk*
salt and sugar to taste
2–3 large eggs
browned bread crumbs
ghee for frying coorkits

Boil the minced meat. Drain. Grind to a fine paste on a curry stone, mortar and pestle or blender.

Heat 2 tablespoons *ghee* in a pan. Fry the minced onion till just turning brown. Add the meat paste, the ginger and powdered *garam masala* and stir-fry for at least 15 minutes. Add salt and sugar to taste.

Remove from fire and mix in the bread soaked in milk. Knead till well mixed. Divide into equal sized portions and shape into 3 inches × 1 inch bolsters or croquettes.

Coat in whisked egg batter and then coat in bread crumbs. Fry over medium heat until brown. Drain and serve.

Variation:
Fish croquettes are also very popular. Boil the fish adding a few bay leaves and a little chopped ginger, garlic and onion to the water. Drain, mash and debone fish. Then proceed as above.

A good accompaniment with: *French fried potatoes, Salad.*

Serves: 4–6

Crumb Chops

6 breast or loin chops should be
    cut keeping two bones per chop
2 tablespoons onion paste
1 teaspoon ginger paste or ½
    teaspoon ginger powder, ½
    teaspoon garlic paste or ¼
    teaspoon garlic powder
1 lime
1 teaspoon vinegar
1 teaspoon worchester sauce
2 eggs with one tablespoon flour
    (beaten together)
½ teaspoon black pepper (optional)
browned bread crumbs
salt to taste
oil for deep frying

Slit the breast/loin chops from the top of the bones till it comes to the portion with the meat. Scrape all the meat down to where the bone joins the meat of the chop. Cut and slowly lever out one bone, leaving the other attached to chop. If the bone appears too long, chop off the top half. With a mallet pound the meat until the chop is double its original size then place on a plate.

Mix onion paste, garlic and ginger together. Coat chops evenly on both sides with this paste.

Squeeze lime, mix the juice with worchester sauce and vinegar in a cup. Pour over the chops. Marinate for at least 2 hours, turning from time to time.

Remove from marinade (do not try and remove any spices which are coated on the chops). Sprinkle a little salt and pepper on both sides of chops.

Dip in egg and flour batter. Place bread crumbs on a grease proof paper. Coat each chop well on either side with crumbs, shaking off excess, if any. Place on another plate and leave the chops covered at least half an hour before frying.

Heat oil in a large fry pan to smoking. Add one or two chops at a time, reduce heat. Simmer over reduced heat turning chops till they are well browned.

A good accompaniment with: *French fried potatoes, salad* and *tomato sauce.*

Serves: 4–6

Fish Moulée

500 gms fish
1/8 teaspoon turmeric
1 medium-sized onion
1/2 inch piece fresh ginger or 1/2
    teaspoon powder ginger
1 fresh coconut (from which two
    cups coconut milk to be ex-
    tracted)
3–4 green chillies
salt to taste
1 teaspoon sugar (optional)
2 tablespoons oil

Wash and drain the fish. Coat fish with turmeric. Heat oil in pan, when smoking add fish. Stir-fry fish 2–3 minutes, add coconut milk and let it come to a simmer. Halve and slice onion fine and add to simmering fish and coconut milk along with green chillies and finely shredded ginger or powdered ginger. Finally add salt and sugar to taste. Bring to brisk boil and cook until liquid is reduced to nearly half. Remove from fire.

Note: If the fish used is soft and flaky, it should be removed from pan after frying. Then proceed as per cooking instructions given. Add fish during last 10 minutes of cooking.

A good accompaniment with: *Rice*

Serves: 4–6

Hilsa Fish Fry

6–8 slices hilsa (palla or bhing)
2 tablespoons ginger paste
4 tablespoons onion paste
1 teaspoon garlic paste
salt to taste
dry bread crumbs
2 tablespoons flour*
1 cup water*
ghee or oil for frying

*blended in a bowl

Place hilsa pieces in a medium-sized bowl or container and very thoroughly and carefully mix in the next 3 ingredients and the salt. Leave for 6 hours (be careful with the salt, as being a dry preparation, it can easily become too salty) in the refrigerator or in any cool place to marinate, turning a few times until half an hour before it is required to be served.

Take hilsa pieces one at a time, recoating each piece with the ingredients in which it has marinated.

Then carefully dip in batter of flour and water which you should have ready in a bowl and finally coat with bread crumbs.

In a frying pan, in very hot *ghee* or oil, fry the hilsa till nicely browned, turning once.

Serve immediately with a cucumber-onion salad and tomato ketchup.

A good accompaniment with: *Salad* and *Tomato Ketchup*

Serves: 3–4

Jhal Ferazi

500 gms boiled or roasted meat,
    cut into cubes
500 gms onions
6 red dry chillies
6 green chillies
2 medium sized potatoes, cut into
    small cubes and fried (optional)
1 teaspoon garlic paste or ½
    teaspoon garlic powder
2 teaspoons ginger paste or 1
    teaspoon ginger powder
2–3 tablespoons oil
1 teaspoon sugar
salt to taste

Break the red chillies in half and remove seeds. Slit the green chillies.

Take 250 gms onions, halve and slice finely. Halve and slice the other 250 gms onions into thicker pieces. Heat oil in a pan to smoking. Add the red chillies and stir-fry for one minute. Add the finely, sliced onions, ginger and garlic. Fry until onions change to light brown but are still soft.

Add meat cubes, thickly sliced onions, green chillies, salt and sugar. Fry this together for 10–15 minutes. If the onions start catching at the bottom of the pan, add a little water and continue cooking until thickly sliced onions are cooked and oil has come to the surface.

If potatoes are added, this should be done at the same time as thickly sliced onions and meat.

This preparation has very little gravy.

A good accompaniment with: *Boiled Rice, Ghee Bhat* or *Porota*

Serves: 4 or 6

Mince Curry

300 gms minced mutton
¼ of a fresh coconut, skinned
   and finely diced
100 gms peas
2 tomatoes, chopped
1 onion, halved and sliced fine
2 onions, minced fine
1 tablespoon turmeric paste
1 teaspoon chilli paste
1½ teaspoons ginger paste
½ teaspoon garlic paste
garam masala (see page 7)
2 bay leaves
3 tablespoons ghee
salt and sugar to taste

Heat the *ghee* in a deep pan. Fry the diced coconut and keep aside.

Add *garam masala* and bay leaves to the hot *ghee*. Fry till spluttering stops.

Add sliced onion and fry to a golden brown.

Add the minced meat. Fry until meat begins to change colour.

Add the minced onion and the *masala* pastes. Continue to fry a good 10–15 minutes. Sprinkle with water, if necessary, to stop meat or *masalas* from catching at the bottom of the pan. When the *masalas* and meat appear blended and *ghee* appears on the surface, add 3–4 cups water. Bring to the boil. Then cover, reduce heat and gently simmer for ½ an hour.

Remove cover. Add peas and mix well.

Cover and simmer another 10–15 minutes or until peas are cooked. Stir from time to time so that the *masalas* or meat do not catch at the bottom of the pan.

Add fried diced coconut. Stir and simmer another 10–15 minutes, by which time the colour of the gravy should have changed and *ghee* come to the surface of the pan.

Remove from fire.

Serve hot

Variation:
Fried diced potatoes may be added at the same time as the coconut to the minced curry. This will increase the servings.

Note: The quantity of water depends on how much gravy you wish to keep.

A good accompaniment with: *Rice, Ghee Bhat* or *Luchi*

Serves: 4

Murgi Cutlet

Chicken Cutlet

1 chicken, legs and breast only
2 cloves garlic*
1 inch piece ginger*
1 onion
1 tablespoon vinegar or lime juice
½ teaspoon black pepper, freshly
   ground
salt to taste
1 large egg**
½ tablespoon flour**
browned bread crumbs
oil or ghee for frying cutlets

*ground to a paste
**blended together

Only chicken legs are supposed to be used in making cutlets but since this is not economical, the breast meat is also used.

Halve the chicken leg from the joint and also halve breast. From the narrower portion of the leg bone scrape meat carefully towards the fleshier portion of the leg and continue doing so until you reach the other end of the bone, the chicken meat falling over it but not off it leaving only a 2-inch portion of the bone with chicken meat. Chop off the balance portion of the leg bone and keep aside. Treat the upper portion of the leg or thigh in a similar fashion.

With a mallet or flat end of a knife flatten the chicken meat shaping into cutlets.

Remove the breast meat from the bone.

Cover the chicken leg bone kept for the purpose, with the breast meat, pushing at least an inch of the bone inside the chicken meat, then fashion into cutlets using a mallet or flat end of a knife.

Rub with the garlic-ginger-onion paste and sprinkle over with salt and vinegar or fresh lime juice. Marinade for a couple of hours at least.

Dip cutlets into egg mixture, and coat with bread crumbs. Dust of excess crumbs, and deep fry in mildly simmering oil or *ghee* until cooked to a golden brown.

A good accompaniment with: *Fried chips Salad* and *Tomato Sauce*.

Serves: 3–4

Mutton Cutlet

500 gms minced mutton
2 onions, minced fine
1 teaspoon ginger paste or
   shredded ginger
2 green chillies, minced very fine
1 tablespoon minced parsley or
   green coriander leaves
1/4 teaspoon black pepper, freshly
   ground
1 egg
2 slices fresh bread, soaked in a
   little milk
salt and sugar to taste
ghee or oil for frying cutlets

Mix together all ingredients and knead together until well blended. Divide into 8 or 10 equal portions. Shape into cutlets approximately a quarter-inch thick.

If the mince mixture is too moist, use a floured board on which to prepare the cutlets.

Heat *ghee* or oil in a frying pan. Fry the cutlets in gently simmering *ghee* until browned and cooked. Drain off excess *ghee*.

Serve hot with french fries or potato chips and tomato ketchup.

A green salad served along with this would complete the meal.

Note.: The cutlets may also be coated with egg-flour mixture and bread crumbs and then fried.

A good accompaniment with: *Salads, boiled vegetables* and *potato fries*.

Serves: 4–6

Mutton Cutlet Curry

8–10 prepared cutlets, fried in
   ghee and allowed to cool
1 onion, halved and sliced fine
1 onion, ground to a paste
1 teaspoon ginger paste
1/2 tablespoon turmeric paste
1 teaspoon chilli paste
1/4 teaspoon garlic paste (optional)
2 tomatoes (optional)
garam masala (see page 7)
2 bay leaves
2 tablespoons ghee
2 cups water
salt and sugar to taste.

Heat the *ghee* in a *dekchi* or pan. Add bay leaves and *garam masala*. Fry 2 minutes. Add sliced onion and cook till brown and then add all the *masala* pastes. Stir-fry 5 minutes sprinkling a little water if necessary.

Add chopped tomatoes and fry until blended in with *masala*.

Add the water. Add salt and sugar to taste. Stir. Cover pan and allow the gravy to come to the boil.

Thereafter simmer for about 10 or 15 minutes or until gravy is reduced by a third.

Slip in the prepared, cooked cutlets. Spoon gravy over.

Gently simmer for about 10 minutes, then remove pan from fire.

Serve hot.

A good accompaniment with: *Rice* or *Porota*

Serves: 4 or 5

Pantaras

Pancakes with Mince filling, crumbed and fried

For Pancake Batter:
1 cup flour
1 cup milk
2 eggs
a pinch baking powder
ghee for frying pancake

For the Filling:
250 gms minced meat
2 onions, chopped fine
½ teaspoon garam masala pow-
*   dered (see page 7)*
⅛ tsp turmeric paste or powder
1 green chilli, minced fine
salt to taste
1 tablespoon ghee

For Coating Batter:
1 tablespoon flour
2 eggs
browned bread crumbs
ghee for frying

In a bowl whisk together the flour, milk and eggs. Add the baking powder and whisk again. Set aside while preparing filling. In a *karai* heat the *ghee*. Add half the minced onion and brown. Add the minced meat, stir-fry until mince changes colour. Add salt, the turmeric paste or powder, the minced green chillies and the *garam masala* powder. Stir and cook another 10 minutes and then add balance minced onion. Stir-fry until the minced meat is well browned and cooked. Sprinkle with water as you fry the mince if it becomes too dry and catches at the bottom of the *karai*.

Remove mince from fire when cooked.

Heat a 6-inch fry pan on the fire. Add a little *ghee*. When this is hot, add two tablespoons of the prepared batter. Swirl pan so that batter is evenly distributed on pan. Cook till it sets. (When the bubbles appear on top of the pancake it is ready to be turned). Fry the other side. Remove from pan after two minutes or so. Prepare all the pancakes in this manner.

Place a pancake on a flat board. Divide the mince into equal portion. With teaspoon place and fill a portion along one end of pancake leaving a good edge on all 3 sides.

First fold the bottom end over pancake filling and then fold in 2 side ends. Roll to the top end. Seal with egg and flour mixture.

Whisk together the egg and flour in a suitable dish. Spread the bread crumbs on a sheet of paper.

Dip the filled pancakes in the egg-flour batter and then coat in crumbs.

Shallow fry crumbed pancakes in a fry pan till lightly browned

Drain well and serve hot.

Note: Use a non-stick fry pan if available.

A good accompaniment with: *Salad* and *Tomato Sauce*

Serves 4–6

Poached Egg in Tomato Gravy

4 eggs
500 gms tomatoes
2 tablespoons ghee
1 onion, ground to a paste
½ tablespoon turmeric paste
1 teaspoon chilli paste
1 teaspoon ginger paste
¼ teaspoon garlic paste (2 cloves)
garam masala (see page 7)
2 bay leaves
salt and sugar to taste
1 tablespoon coriander leaves,
    chopped

Chop tomatoes and rub through strainer into bowl. Add water, if necessary, to make 2 full cups juice.

Heat *ghee* in *karai*. Add bay leaves and *garam masala* and fry till spluttering stops.

Add all the pasted *masalas* and fry 5–7 minutes sprinkling with water, if necessary.

Add 2 cups tomato juice, salt and sugar to taste and bring to the boil. After 5 minutes reduce heat to a medium simmer.

Break one egg at a time on to tomato gravy. Poach eggs in tomato gravy spooning gravy over eggs until eggs have hardened and gravy is reduced to nearly half or less.

To serve, spoon eggs carefully into serving dish, pouring gravy into dish from one side.

Sprinkle with chopped coriander leaves.

A good accompaniment with: *Rice, Ghee Bhat* or *Porota*

Serves: 2–3

Pork Vindaloo

500–750 gms pork, preferably on
   the lean side
3–4 tablespoons mustard oil
½ tablespoon turmeric
2 teaspoons chilli paste
1½ tablespoons mustard paste
½ tablespoon cummin paste
½ tablespoon ginger paste
1 teaspoon garlic paste
2 tablespoons vinegar
1 teaspoon salt
1–2 teaspoons sugar

Heat oil in a *dekchi* or pan till smoking hot. Add all the *masala* pastes and stir-fry until *masalas* are well cooked and have changed colour. Sprinkle with the vinegar as you fry the *masalas* using all the vinegar.

Add the pork and salt to taste. Stir and cook until the natural juices of the pork are all absorbed.

Add 2–3 cups water. Cover pan and simmer over low heat until pork is tender.

Adjust seasoning, adding sugar to taste.

Remove from fire.

Duck Vinadaloo
Jointed pieces of duck can be substituted for pork and cooked in the same way.

Brinjal Vindaloo
Cooking time: 5–10 minutes.
   This is not an Anglo-Indian dish, but a Bengali adaptation using the *vindaloo* paste. Small brinjals halved are fried in oil and put aside, then added to the *masala* pastes when ready.

A good accompaniment with: *Rice*

Serves: 4–6

Smoked Hilsa

1 hilsa (1 kg-1¼ kg)
4 tablespoons worcester sauce
4–6 tablespoons salad
   oil / sunflower oil
1 tablespoon anchovy sauce
1 tablespoon tomato sauce
1 teaspoon pepper
1 teaspoon caramelised sugar
salt to taste
khoi and sand for smoking

Fillet fish into 2 fillets. (Head and bones can be used for *chhanchra*). Mix together all other ingredients and marinate fish in this for at least one hour—preferably longer.

On a *tawa* put a thick layer of sand. This is to prevent *khoi* from burning too quickly. Over this, put a double layer of *khoi*. Place *tawa* on high heat. When *khoi* starts smoking, place one fillet carefully on the *khoi* skin side down and spoon a little of the marinade over the fish using a large deep *karai, dekchi* or pan, invert over the *tawa* to cover both *tawa* and cooking ring. Reduce heat slightly but maintain a steady smoke from *tawa*. Uncover after 10 minutes and baste with a little more of the marinade. Cover and cook for further 10 minutes. Remove *tawa* from heat and with a fish slice carefully lift off the fish and place on a board. Ignore any *khoi* sticking to the skin. Scrape off all sand and *khoi* from *tawa* and repeat again with layers of sand and *khoi* to cook the other fillet. If *tawa* is big enough, both fillets can be cooked at the same time. Allow fish to cool sufficiently to handle.

Deboning:
This sounds more difficult than it actually is. Use 2 knives; with one make 3 cuts along length of fillet to the skin but not cutting it along its natural divisions—it is quite simple to cut along these. Starting from one side, using one knife placed along the cut to hold fillet in place, use other knife to gently push fish off the skin, working from the cut sideways. Fine bones will be seen protruding from both cut edges. Carefully pull these out. Using same procedure, separate the sections of fillet from skin. Each time remove the bones from the newly exposed cut edges. When all pieces have been deboned, lift pieces carefully on the serving dish, placing them to reform the shape of the fillet. Reheat gently in oven and serve hot with a border of finely cut crisp potato straws.

Although the traditional way of cooking has been given above which imparts a typical smoky flavour to the fish, the cooking can be greatly simplified without losing too much of its character.

Place marinated fillet in a roasting pan and bake in a medium hot oven for 20–30 minutes.

Baste with a little of the marinade twice during cooking.

Debone and serve as for traditional method.

This dish is usually served as a starter and the quantity given will serve 4. It is normally eaten on its own.

Tomato Farci

Stuffed Tomatoes

8–10 medium to large tomatoes
mince filling as for Pantaras
(see page 166)

Cut a slice across the stem-ends of the tomatoes and keep aside. Remove all pulp and seeds from inside of tomatoes. Discard these.

Stuff the tomato cups with the prepared mince, fill right to the brim. Cover with the cut tomato slices kept aside for this purpose. Place in lightly oiled oven-proof dish. Cover with lid or foil and bake in a preheated 325°F oven for 45 minutes or until tomatoes are cooked.

Alternatively, place 2 or 3 *farcis* in a frying pan and fry in *ghee* over a gentle flame until tomatoes are cooked.

Drain off *ghee* and serve.

Variation:
A fish or *chhana (panir)* filling may be substituted.

A good accompaniment with: *Fried chipped potatoes, Salad*

Serves: 4–5

AMBOL, TAUK, ACHAR

CHUTNEYS AND PICKLES

Chutneys and Pickles

I would like to mention the distinction between *tauk* or *ambal* and *chutney* and *achar*.

A *tauk* or *ambal* is generally prepared for the midday meal. This has a sweet-sour light gravy and is made with green mango or any other fruit, imparting sourness. It is served cold and eaten on the day it is prepared.

Chutney is a thicker and more syrupy version of *tauk*. It can be kept for a few days. The quantity of sugar added is at the preference of the individual—depending on whether a sweet or a tart chutney is preferred.

Bengali pickles or *achar* are generally mustard oil based with spices and are either cooked or sun-dried to mature. These can be preserved for a period of time.

Aam Jhol

Green Mango Chutney with light gravy

2 large or 4 medium sized green
  mangoes, preferably seedless
1/4 teaspoon turmeric paste
1 teaspoon mustard oil
1/8 teaspoon panch phoran
3–4 cups water
1 teaspoon salt (adjust to taste)
2 tablespoons sugar (adjust to
  taste)

Peel and cut the mangoes into narrow strips lengthwise. Mix in the quarter teaspoon turmeric paste.

Heat the teaspoon of oil in a *karai* or pan and when this is really hot, add the *panch phoran*.

Immediately the *phoran* stops spluttering, add the mango slices and fry lightly for a couple of minutes or so.

Then pour in the water.

Add salt to taste and sugar according to preference and sourness of the mangoes. *Aam Jhol* should taste sweet-sour. Simmer gently until mangoes are soft but not pulpy.

Remove from fire and cool.

Aam Jhol should be served as cold as possible. There should be quite a large quantity of gravy. Delightful when served in teacups at the end of a meal.

Serves: 4–6

Aam Kasondi

Mango Pickle with Mustard

1 kg. green mangoes
*250 gms coarse salt
50 gms fresh ginger, ground to
  paste
25 gms dry red chillies, freshly
  powdered
150 gms mustard seed, freshly
  powdered
50 gms ripe seedless tamarind
250 gms mustard oil
salt to taste

*Please use only ordinary sea salt
and not iodised salt. Iodised salt is
not a preservative

Peel and de-seed the mangoes and slice into equal sized pieces. Mix in the coarse salt. Place in a wooden or porcelain bowl and leave in the sun for a couple of days or until the mango pieces are quite soft.

Lightly sqeeze and drain off the juice accumulated in the bowl after two days of sunning.

Now add to the mangoes all the spices, the ripe tamarind and salt. Mix thoroughly.

In a large aluminium *karai* or pan heat the oil until a blue haze appears.

Add the spiced mango pieces.

Stir and mix thoroughly with the oil and remove from fire. Allow to cool and then pour into an airtight glass or earthenware jar. Will keep for—2 months.

Makes: 2 medium or 1 large jar

Aamer Chutney (1)

Mango Chutney

4 large green mangoes, preferably
   without stones
1 teaspoon slaked lime (chuna)
1 tablespoon mustard oil
3–4 whole dry red chillies
1/4 teaspoon panch phoran
2 cups water
1/2 cup sugar
salt to taste
1 tablespoon cummin seed*
1 teaspoon mustard seed*
1 dry red chilli*

*dry-fried and powdered

Cut the mango in 4 or 6 lengthwise, without peeling. Add *chuna* to a bowl full of water and soak the pieces of mango in this for 3 to 4 hours. Thereafter, drain the mango from the *chuna* water: Wash thoroughly and dry with small clean towel.

Heat the oil in a *karai* or pan. When oil is smoking hot, fry the mango slices in this until lightly browned. Remove from pan and keep aside. To the same pan add the dry red chillies and the *panch phoran* and when spluttering stops, pour in the two cups water, the sugar and a little salt.

Let this come to the boil and add the mango slices. Adjust seasoning.

Simmer over medium heat until the sugar syrup thickens. When the syrup has thickened to the desired consistency, pour into serving bowl and sprinkle the dry ground spices over chutney.

If liked, raisins can also be added.

Will keep a week or more in the refrigerator.

Note: The consistency of the chutney is according to preference. Generally, it has a thick syrup gravy.

A good accompaniment with: *Rice, Luchi* or *eaten separately*

Serves: 4–6

Aamer Chutney (2)

Mango Chutney

6 large green mangoes, preferably
   without stones
2 cups sugar
8 cups water
6 dry red chillies*
2-inch piece of ginger*
2 cloves garlic*

*Ground to paste in vinegar
salt

Cut the mangoes lengthwise into 4 to 6 pieces. Rub with a little salt and keep aside for a while.

Heat 8 cups of water in a large pan.

Add the sugar and bring to the boil.

Remove any scum that may appear. Continue simmering for about 10–15 minutes before adding all the *masala* pastes.

Simmer until water is reduced and the syrup has thickened. Add the pieces of mangoes.

On addition of the sliced mangoes, the syrup will again become quite light because of the water from mangoes.

Continue simmering until syrup thickens again, mangoes are cooked and the chutney has thickened.

Note: Grinding *masala* in vinegar helps preserve the chutney better.

Served at end of meal

Serves: 6–8

Aamer Misti Achar

Sweet Hot Mango Chutney

6 large half-ripe green mangoes
1 cup vinegar
1 cup sugar
2 tablespoons raisins, soaked and
   washed in water
2-inch piece of ginger, cut in
   julienne strips
1 teaspoon red chilli powder
3–4 whole red chillies

Peel the mangoes and discard stones. Cut into thin slices lengthwise.

Wash and keep soaked in water for a while. Remove and dry thoroughly with a towel.

Heat the vinegar in a pan.

Add the sliced mangoes and ginger. When it comes to a boil, add the sugar, chilli powder and whole dry red chillies.

Stir continuously with a wooden spoon until mangoes are quite cooked and syrup is thick.

Remove from fire. Cool and bottle.

Will keep for 1–2 months

Served at end of meal or with meal as preferred

Makes: 2 medium or 1 large jar

Alubokhara Chutney

Prune Chutney

100 gms alubokhara/prunes
100 gms raisins
100 gms dates (seedless)
1/4 teaspoon panch phoran
3–4 red chillies
1/4 teaspoon turmeric
3 or 4 tablespoons sugar
salt to taste
1 1/2 cups water

Clean and wash the *alubokhara*, dates and raisins. Soak in water to cover for several hours.

Heat oil in a *karai*. Add *panch phoran* and the red chillies broken in half. Stir and fry until spluttering stops.

Add turmeric paste. Stir and add *alubokhara*, raisins and dates with the water used for soaking (not exceeding one and a half cups).

Stir and simmer.

Add the sugar and salt to taste.

Simmer until *alubokhara* is cooked and the chutney is quite thick.

This particular chutney is served at weddings and on special occasions.

A good accompaniment with: *Papor (Padadum) with the meal or on its own*

Serves: 12

Anaras Chutney

Pineapple Chutney

a quarter of a large pineapple
1 teaspoon oil
1/8 tsp mustard seed
1 inch piece ginger, finely
  shredded
1/2 tablespoon raisins, cleaned
  and soaked in water
2 bay leaves
2–4 tablespoons sugar
salt to taste
1 1/2 cups water

Discard the hard core of the pineapple. Peel and remove the 'eyes'. Dice fine.

Heat oil in a *karai*. Add the mustard seeds and when spluttering stops, add the diced pineapple. Stir and fry for 5 minutes or so, add salt to taste.

Add water and sugar as preferred.

Add bay leaves, raisins and shredded ginger. Simmer until chutney has thickened to required consistency.

Note: If using canned pineapple, adjust cooking time and quantity of sugar. Some vinegar may also be added.

A good accompaniment with: *Rice, Ghee Bhat, Porota* or *at end of meal*

Serves: 4–6

Choto Chingri Sambal

Sweet and Sour Shrimp Chutney

250 gms shrimps/sardines/small
   fish
50 gms red pumpkin
6 ladies' fingers/bhindi
1 sweet potato
1/4 teaspoon turmeric paste
1/4 tsp chilli paste
fresh raw tamarind or a small
   lump ripe tamarind—extract
   juice (see general instructions)
salt to taste
2 tablespoons sugar or as required
1/8 teaspoon mustard seeds
2 whole dry red chillies
1/2 tablespoon oil
4 cups water

Shell and clean the shrimps. Dice the vegetables into small pieces.

Heat oil in a pan and when smoking hot, add the mustard seeds and red chillies. When mustard seeds stop spluttering, add the vegetables.

Stir-fry a few minutes and then add the shrimps, coated with the turmeric and chilli paste. Stir-fry until shrimps begin to change colour.

Mix the tamarind juice with the water and pour into the pan. Add salt to taste and the sugar. Stir and bring to the boil.

Simmer until vegetables are soft but whole.

Remove from fire, cook and serve. Should be served at room temperature.

Variation:
Tamarind juice may be replaced by approximately 2 tablespoons vinegar and vegetables may also be varied.

A good accompaniment with: *Rice*

Serves: 6–8

Lankar Achar

Green Chilli Pickle

1 kg green chillies, cut in ¼ inch
  rounds
50 gms fresh ginger, ground to a
  paste
50 gms fresh ginger, shredded or
  minced very fine
50 gms chilli powder
100 gms garlic, ground to paste
30 gms turmeric powder
60 gms mustard seeds, a teaspoon
  set aside and the balance
  ground to a fine paste.
2 cups vinegar
3 cups mustard oil
salt to taste
2 tablespoons sugar

Add about a level tablespoon salt to the chillies, mix and set aside for a few hours or overnight.

Grind the *masala* paste with vinegar instead of water.

Heat half the oil to smoking in a pan and fry the chillies in this for about 10 minutes. Remove chillies to another dish. Add three-quarters of the remaining oil to the pan. Allow this to become smoking hot. Add the teaspoon of mustard seed and when it stops sputtering, add the shredded ginger. Fry for a minute and then add the other *masala* pastes, ginger and garlic.

Fry for a good 10 minutes or more until the *masalas* change colour, then add the remaining vinegar and 2 tablespoons of sugar.

Add the fried chillies to the *masalas* in the pan, fry for another 10 minutes.

Adjust seasoning. Just before removing from fire, add the remaining oil and mix well.

Cool and store in jars.

Note: More sugar can be added if a sweet-hot pickle is preferred.

Please use non-iodised salt (ordinary sea salt) for pickles. Iodised salt is *not* a preservative.

A good accompaniment with: *Any food*

Make: 2 medium jars

Lau Ba Peper Chutney

Bottle Gourd or Papaya Chutney

250 gms lau (dudhi) or raw
  papaya
a walnut sized ball of ripe
  tamarind without seeds
1½ cups water
1 tablespoon raisins
¼ teaspoon mustard seeds
3–4 dry whole red chillies
2 teaspoons mustard oil
salt and sugar to taste
1 teaspoon flour mixed with a little water
1 tablespoon mango-ginger
  (amada) paste

Peel the *lau*/papaya and remove seeds. Slice fine into julienne strips.

Boil in water to cover until just done. Drain and dry with a towel.

Soak the tamarind in 1½ cups water. Mix thoroughly, sieve and keep the liquid aside in a bowl.

Clean, wash and soak raisins. Dry and keep aside.

Heat the oil in a *karai* or pan till blue haze appears.

Add the mustard seeds and dry red chillies, broken in half.

Stir-fry a couple of minutes and add the *lau*/papaya. The *lau*/papaya will give off some water. Cook over high heat until water is absorbed.

Now add the tamarind water, raisins, sugar to taste and adjust salt.

Simmer over medium heat until gravy is thickened considerably.

To bring it to the right consistency, add the flour mixed with a little water.

Bring to boil, simmer 5 minutes; mix in mango-ginger paste and remove from fire.

Serve when quite cold.

Note: This chutney is sweet and therefore sugar should be added accordingly.

A good accompaniment with: *Rice*

Serves: 8–12

Maacher Dimer Tauk

Fish Roe Chutney

*250 gms fish roe (the roe of any
large fish will do but best with
roe of rui, katla, mrigel and
hilsa)*
1 teaspoon turmeric
2–3 teaspoons mustard oil
½ teaspoon mustard seed
3–4 dry whole red chillies
*1 tablespoon cummin seed**
*1 dry whole red chilli**
salt and sugar to taste

roasted and powdered

Medium sized ball of ripe tamarind with seeds removed, soaked in 2 cups water.

Cut the fish roe into inch pieces and coat with the turmeric paste and a little salt.

Heat the oil in a *karai* or pan and add the mustard seeds and halved dry red chillies.

Stir-fry a couple of minutes and then add the fish roe. Fry the fish roe in the oil until browned. Add a sprinkling of water if the pan is too dry while frying.

Pour in the tamarind juice through a sieve. Add sugar as liked and adjust the salt.

Simmer over medium heat until gravy is reduced to half. Add the powdered spices, stir and cook another 5 minutes and remove from fire.

Serve cold.

A good accompaniment with: *Rice*

Serves: 6–8

Tetul Gola

Tamarind Pickle

1 kg ripe tamarind
4–6 cups water or as required
25 gms dry red chillies, freshly
    powdered
100 gms mustard seeds, roasted
    and powdered
1 teaspoon peppercorns powdered
250 gms sugar (approx)
250 gms mustard oil
*25 gms salt (approx)

*Please use ordinary sea salt and
    not iodised salt. Iodised salt is
    not a preservative.

Wash the tamarind and soak in water to cover for several hours.

Using a fine muslin cloth, strain the tamarind juice into a porcelain or wooden bowl.

Cover with another piece of muslin and leave in the sun for a minimum of two days when tamarind juice should have thickened considerably.

Add all the prepared powdered *masalas* to the tamarind juice and mix well.

Then add sugar, salt to taste and mix again.

Then add some of the mustard oil and mix again. Place in the sun.

Add some mustard oil everyday, for 5 days, (using up all the mustard oil) and sunning every day. Stir well everyday. Continue to sun for a further 5 days.

After this, do not stir until the 10th day.

By this time, the *Tetul Gola* should be ready for serving or bottling.

Bottle in clean dry jars. Will keep for several months. Sun from time to time and add a little extra mustard oil, if dry.

Note: The amount of sugar used depends on the tartness of the tamarind. The quantities of chilli and pepper powder makes this a medium-hot chutney, and these spices can be adjusted to taste.

A good accompaniment with: *any food*

Makes: 2 medium jars or 1 large jar

Tomato Chutney

250 gms tomatoes, cut in four
1 inch piece ginger, peeled and
    cut in julienne strips
½ teaspoon red chilli powder
1 tablespoon raisins, soaked and
    cleaned in water
⅛ teaspoon panch phoran
1 teaspoon mustard oil
salt and sugar to taste

Heat mustard oil in a pan.

Add *panch phoran* to hot oil and fry till spluttering stops.

Add chopped tomatoes. Stir well.

Add salt, cover and simmer 10 minutes.

Remove cover. Add julienned ginger strips, red chilli powder and raisins.

Add 2–3 tablespoons sugar and a cup of water.

Continue simmering until tomato chutney has thickened and is cooked.

Serve cold.

A good accompaniment with: *Rice, Luchi*

Serves: 6

Tomato Kasondi

Sweet Hot Tomato Pickle with Mustard

	For 2 kg	For 5 kg
Tomato	2 kgs	5 kgs
Mustard oil	2 cups	5 cups
Vinegar	2 cups	5 cups
Garlic	35 gms	85 gms
Turmeric	20 gms	50 gms
Ginger	35 gms	85 gms
Chilli	20 gms	50 gms
Cummin seeds	20 gms	50 gms
Mustard seeds	20 gms	50 gms
Sugar	½ cup (approx)	1 cup

*Salt to taste

Grind all the *masalas* with vinegar to a very fine paste (including garlic and ginger).

In a suitable sized pan, heat mustard oil to smoking and add all the *masala* paste.

Fry for a good 10–15 minutes adding vinegar if necessary so that *masala* does not catch at the bottom of the pan.

Cut tomato in four and add to the pan. Mix with the *masala* and fry for another 5–10 minutes.

Then add the remaining vinegar, salt to taste and sugar.

Simmer over very slow fire for about 1½–2 hours or until oil surfaces.

Remove pan from heat. Cool and pour *kasondi* into air-tight jars.

Will keep several months.

Note: The quantity of oil is approximate. To preserve the *kasondi* more oil may have to be added in the final stages of cooking.

*Please use ordinary sea salt for pickles, and not iodised salt. Iodised salt is *not* a preservative

A good accompaniment with: *Any food*

Makes: 4 large jars or 8–10 medium jars

Mango Murabba

Sweet Mango Preserve

6 raw mangoes, preferably
    without stones
½ teaspoon chuna (slaked lime)
4 cups sugar
6–8 cloves
4-inch piece cinnamon, broken
    into piece
6–8 green cardamoms, peeled,
    seeds extracted
2 tablespoons raisins, soaked in
    water and washed clean
2–3 cups water
salt to taste

Peel and dice the mangoes. Prick the diced mangoes with a fork.

Add the *chuna* to water and soak the mangoes in this for several hours (6–8 hours).

Remove and wash thoroughly in several changes of water. Place the diced mangoes in a pan with water to cover. Add a little salt.

Bring water to the boil and then remove from fire. Drain.

Dry mangoes as much as possible.

In a *dekchi* bring to the boil the water and sugar. Remove the scum that forms on the surface of the syrup.

Add the mangoes and continue cooking.

Add the cinnamon, cloves and cardamom seeds. Also the raisins. Mix well.

Simmer the mangoes in the sugar syrup, stirring from time to time, until quite soft. There should only be a very thick syrup left.

Remove from fire. Cool and bottle.

Will keep several months.

A good accompaniment with: *any food*

Makes: 1 medium bottle or jar

Topa Kooler Ambal

Plum Chutney with gravy

250 gms topa kool (Indian plum)
1 teaspoon mustard oil
2–3 whole red chillies
a pinch mustard seed
2–3 tablespoons sugar
3 cups water
salt to taste

Remove stems from *kool*. Press in the centre and de-seed. Wash well and keep aside.

Heat oil in *karai*. Add whole red chillies and mustard seeds. When spluttering stops, add *kool*. Stir and cook about 5 minutes adding salt to taste.

Add water and sugar. Simmer for about 15 minutes, then remove from fire.

Cool and serve.

Note: Sugar is used according to taste. More sugar can be added if a sweeter *ambal* is preferred.

Served at end of meal

Serves: 6–8

JAL KHABAR

SNACKS

Jalkhabar
Snacks

The Bengali cuisine is also rich in the preparation of savouries and sweets eaten during elevenses and afternoon tea. It was a daily ritual for the women of the family to prepare *Jalkhabar*. For most young girls, an introduction into the kitchen started with an essay at some of the simple preparations.

This daily ritual is no longer practicable, but on special occasions when guests are expected to tea, we still prefer to make *jalkhabar* at home rather than serve shop bought snacks.

Apart from the recipes given in this section, for a more substantial snack, *Radhaballobi* or *Luchi* with *Alu-dom* or any or the *Ghugnis* can be served.

Alu Kabli

300 grams potatoes
4–6 tablespoons lime juice
1/2–1 teaspoon chilli powder
salt to taste
2 tablespoons coriander leaves,
  chopped

Wash potatoes but do not peel. Boil until just tender. Do not over boil. Cooc slightly and peel. Cut into thick slices or 1/2 inch cubes. Allow to cool thoroughly before tossing in all other ingredients, taking care not to break up the potato pieces. Serve cold.

Serves: 4

Chiré Bhaja

Fried Flaked Rice

1 cup chiré (flaked rice)
1/2 cup oil or ghee
salt and pepper to taste

Optional additions:
100 gms cooked peas
1/8 tsp turmeric
100 gms potatoes fried in julienne
    strips
2 tablespoons chopped coriander
    leaves
1 tablespoon chopped green chillies
100 gms. roasted peanuts

Heat oil to smoking point. Add *chiré* all together and fry stirring constantly. *Chiré* should fluff up to twice the size but should not brown. Remove from heat and mix in other optional ingredients except turmeric. Return to heat and fry two minutes. Drain oil. Serve hot.

If turmeric is used, it should be mixed with the chiré and cooked at the same time.

Note: To store, cool thoroughly and keep in airtight tin. Keeps for 1 week.

Caution: Chiré *cooks* very fast and burns easily. Use a large wire strainer to remove chiré from the hot oil.

Serves: 4–6

Chirér Pulao

Flaked Rice Pilaff

1 cup chiré (flaked rice)
100 gms. potatoes sliced and fried
    crisp
100 gms onion sliced fine and
    fried
8 green chillies, slit
150 gms roasted peanuts
25 gms raisins
salt to taste
1/4 cup oil
coriander leaves to garnish

Wash *chiré* and drain immediately, gently squeezing out excess water. Heat oil to smoking point. Add *chiré* and fry for 2 minutes. Add all other ingredients and fry for 5 minutes or till *chiré* is cooked. Garnish with chopped coriander leaves.

Serve immediately.

A whole broken egg added to the *chiré* while cooking gives extra nourishment.

Note: Texture of the *pulao* should be flaky and not mushy.

Serves: 4–6

Elo Jhelo

250 gms flour*
2 tablespoons ghee*
1 cup water*
ghee for deep frying
3 cups sugar**
1 cup water**

*Mix together with just sufficient
  water to form dough. Knead
  until soft and pliable.
**To be made into thick syrup

Divide dough into equal but small portions. Then form into balls.

Roll out with rolling pin on floured board into oval ⅛-inch thick.

With a knife cut away two side edges and also cut across the top and the bottom to straighten and form oblongs of dough.

With the knife make lengthwise slits in the oblongs of dough. Be careful to keep the top and bottom edges of the dough intact.

Lift from board and lightly fold lengthwise. Press the top and the bottom ends to seal (if necessary use a little water) but see that the centre of the dough is quite loose.

Holding top and bottom of folded oblong of dough between the thumb and forefinger of the two hands, move hands in opposite directions to give a twist to the dough similar to a cheese straw.

When all the portions of dough are formed into Elo-Jhelos, collect all the cutaway pieces and reform these into balls and make as many more Elo-Jhelos as possible.

Heat *ghee* in *karai* or pan and deep fry until lightly browned and crisp.

Remove and drain off excess *ghee* by placing on absorbent paper.

As you finish frying the Elo-Jhelos, prepare the thick syrup.

While syrup is hot, place Elo-Jhelos in the syrup a few at a time. Coat well with syrup and set aside on a flat dish until sugar syrup has set on the Elo-Jhelos.

The Elo-Jhelos are ready for serving as soon as the sugar syrup has set.

Serves: 8–12

Jibé-Goja

Sugar-coated Pastry

250 gms flour
2 tbs ghee
a pinch baking powder
ghee for deep frying
1 cup sugar*
½ cup water*

*boiled together to make very thick syrup

Sift together the flour and baking powder. Mix in the *ghee* and knead to a pliable dough with a little water. Divide into 12 or 14 portions.

On a floured pastry board, using a rolling pin, roll out into ovals about ⅛-inch thick. Make several small slashes on the ovals of dough with the tip of knife or prick with a fork.

Heat *ghee* in pan and deep fry *Goja* until lightly browned and crisp. Remove from *ghee* with slotted spoon, drain off excess oil on absorbent paper.

Then coat lightly by dipping in in the prepared syrup, leaving the goja to soak for one minute.

Put on a flat dish and allow syrup to set on *Goja*.

Serves: 6–12

Matarsutir Kochuri

Luchis stuffed with Peas

For dough:
500 gms flour
2 tablespoons ghee
1/2 teaspoon salt
a pinch bicarbonate of soda
1 cup water approximately

For filling:
100 gms green peas
1 teaspoon aniseed
1/8 teaspoon onion seeds
1/8 tsp black pepper, powdered
1/2 teaspoon salt
1/2 teaspoon sugar
1 tablespoon ghee
ghee for deep-frying kochuris

To make the filling, shell peas and grind to a dry paste. Heat *ghee*, add the pea paste and all the *masalas*, black pepper, salt and a half teaspoon sugar. Stir thoroughly until peas and *masalas* are well blended. Remove from fire. Keep aside till dough is ready.

Sieve the flour and salt. Mix in the bicarbonate of soda. Add *ghee* and enough water to make dough. Knead till dough is soft and pliable. Divide into 16 portions and round into balls.

Stuff each ball with a little of the filling as described under *Radhaballobhi* (see p. 22). Seal carefully and roll out into rounds the same size as *luchis* but a little thicker.

Deep fry as for *luchi* but fry each side a little longer.

Excellent on its own but may be served with Aludom.

Serves: 8

Mohon Bhog

Semolina Pudding

1 cup suji (semolina)
1/2 cup sugar
1 cup milk or milk and water
1/4 cup ghee or butter
2 tablespoons raisins
2 bay leaves
2 cardamoms
2 tablespoons any type unsalted
   nuts (optional)

Heat *ghee* in a *karai*. Add suji and fry gently till golden brown. Add all other ingredients and gently stir-fry till well mixed.

Cover and cook on low heat till all the milk is absorbed and the *suji* grains have swollen. A light glaze of ghee should be on the surface.

Preferably served hot.

A sweet which is served on its own at elevenses or tea.

Serves: 4

Murir Moa

Crunchy puffed Rice Balls

250 gms muri/puffed rice
500 gms gur/cane jaggery
½ cup water

Break *gur* into pieces, add water and cook gently till dissolved. Bring to boil and cook till mixture thickens and darkens in colour. Test for hard ball consistency. Stir in *muri*. Remove from heat.

Then, with hands moistened in cold water, pick up one handful and form quickly into ball and put aside. Repeat this process, stirring mixture occasionally in between.

Keeping a bowl of water by the side of the cooker is a help. A *karai* gives easier access to the contents than a saucepan. The key to this preparation is the speed at which the balls are made.

Variations:
Moa can also be made from puffed wheat, popped corn and rice flakes.

A sweet which is a favourite with children and adults alike. Is eaten any time of the day.

Serves: 4–6

Nimki

250 gms. flour
3 tablespoons ghee
1 teaspoon salt
½ cup water approximately
½ teaspoon onion seeds
oil for deep frying
flour for rolling

Sieve flour and salt together.

Rub in *ghee*. Add just enough water to make a firm dough. Knead well. Then knead in onion seeds. Divide into 24 portions. Roll out each portion thinly into 4" diameter circles. Flour both sides lightly. Shake off excess flour and fold into quarters. Prick well and deep fry in hot oil.

Drain and serve.

To store—Cool thoroughly and keep in airtight container.

Like a savoury biscuit. Can be eaten at any time.

Serves: 4–6

Shingara

For the Pastry:
250 gms flour
2 tablespoons ghee
1/8 tsp of salt
1/2 cup water approximately
oil for deep frying

For the Filling:
100 gms cauliflower in tiny
  flowerets
100 gms potato diced
100 gms shelled peas
50 gms onion, sliced fine
2 tablespoons oil
1/8 tsp of turmeric
1/4 teaspoon cummin powder
1/4 teaspoon coriander powder
1/8 tsp of chilli powder
salt to taste
1/4 teaspoon sugar
1/4 teaspoon ginger paste or
  ginger powder

Filling:
Heat oil and fry all ingredients over low heat till cooked. If necessary, add a little water. Set aside and allow to cool completely.

Pastry:
Rub *ghee* into sieved flour and salt to resemble semolina. Add enough water to make soft, pliable dough. Knead thoroughly till dough comes clean off the board. Cover and allow to rest for at least 1/2 hour. Divide into 12 equal portions and roll out like *luchi* into 4" diameter circles. Cut each circle into half. Taking one half, form a hollow cone by folding along cut side and bringing upto the middle. Overlap the two sides slightly and seal by wetting edges.

Fill each cone three-quarters full with prepared filling. Wet along the open mouth of the cone and seal. Pinch the edge all along and twist at corners. The finished *shingara* is triangular in shape.

Heat oil till very hot and gently slide in a few *shingaras* at a time. Fry till golden brown. Remove with slotted spoon and drain excess oil.

Variations:
Shingaras can be made with any cooked filling of your choice—meat, fish, chicken etc. Ensure that the filling is dry.

Serves: 6

Tel Muri

200 gms muri (puffed rice)
3–4 tablespoons mustard oil
4 tablespoons onion, finely
  chopped
2 green chillies, finely chopped,
  preferably with seeds removed
salt to taste

Mix all ingredients together in a bowl and serve at once. Muri should be crisp when mixed. Mixture will get soft if left standing for long.

Serves: 4–6

MISHTI

SWEETS

Misti
Sweets

It was many years ago that every household made its own sweet dishes. The principles of economy and the skill required for the popular preparations led to families specialising in confectionery-making, where expertise was handed down from father to son.

The community, known as *Moiras*, has developed sweet-making into a fine art and specialities like *rosogolla* and *sandesh* made at home can seldom match the better qualities available in confectionery shops. The quality of these sweets made of *chhana* (fresh *panir* or cottage cheese), depend on the quality of milk available and my experience today is that better quality Bengali sweets are available outside Bengal.

Misti Doi or sweetened yogurt is a must for the Bengali. Made with thickened milk and well set, it is a delicacy and most popularly eaten with *sandesh*. The famous *rosogolla* is seldom prepared at home. It needs experience to get the right degree of sponginess and quite often, the first few attempts result in a *rosogolla* with a hard core. Nevertheless, a recipe has been included for the adventurous.

Bhapa Doi

Steamed Sweetened Yogurt

1 tin condensed milk
400 gms unsweetened yogurt
nuts and raisins—to decorate

Heat oven to 400°F. Put a kettle of water to boil.

Whip condensed milk and yogurt till smooth and fluffy. Take care not to overbeat or else yogurt will emit water. Pour into a shallow ceramic or pyrex oven-proof dish. Decorate with nuts and raisins.

Set the dish on a baking tray. Pour hot water, half way up the dish. Bake for half an hour or till skewer inserted comes out clean.

Colour
A beigy pink
Texture
Smooth, cuts clean with a spoon
Flavour
Caramel, sweet and sour

Serves: 8–10

Bondé

250 gms besan (chick-pea flour)
a pinch bicarbonate of soda
50 gms powdered rice or rice flour
1¼—1½ cups of water, ghee or
*   oil for deep frying*
4 cups sugar
4 cups water for syrup

First make the syrup. Heat together the 4 cups sugar and 4 cups water. Bring to the boil and simmer until you have a syrup of medium consistency. Remove from fire and allow to cool.

To make the *Bondé*, blend together the *besan* and water. Mix in the powdered rice and bicarbonate of soda. Keep aside until *ghee* is smoking hot.

Through a *jhanjri* or a flat round slotted spoon with round slots, pour the *besan* mixture on to the hot *ghee*, little at a time until the surface of the *ghee* is covered with very small balls or *Bondé*. Fry until crisp but not brown.

Remove from *ghee* with slotted spoon. Drain on paper for short while but while still hot immerse in the prepared syrup.

Continue in the above manner until all the mixture is used.

After the *Bondé* is soaked in the syrup for a while, remove with slotted spoon and spread on a flat dish.

To serve, place in a bowl.

A good accompaniment with: *Doi*.

Serves: 4–6

Payesh

Rice Pudding with a difference

Traditional *payesh* is made by reducing milk to half its original volume, sweetened with jaggery or sugar.

To this is added varied ingredients such as rice, semolina, flaked rice, vermicelli, fresh corn, etc. Though the traditional *payesh* is made with rice, there is no limit to what one can do.

I remember an innovative non-Bengali cook, enthusiastic to make a new *payesh*, produced "*Spaghetti Payesh*" much to our horror. Let me till you, it was good.

Traditional Payesh:

2 litres milk
4 tablespoons sugar
2–3 tablespoons rice (washed well
*   and dried on plate)*
a few raisins
a few almonds finely sliced
*   (optional)*

Heat milk in a large pan. Simmer until reduced to three-quarters its original volume. Add washed rice. Add sugar when rice is tender and continue cooking until milk is reduced to half its original volume. Add raisins and finely sliced almonds. Cool and serve.

Variation:
Natun Gurer Payesh
During the winter months, fresh palm jaggery is available in Bengal. This is a delicacy and is often used in making *payesh*. When jaggery is used, it is stirred in after taking *payesh* off the fire as it will otherwise curdle.
OR
Add 2 tablespoons sugar before removing from fire. Add the jaggery to taste after removing from fire.

Jethima's Payesh for a Crowd

Aunt's Rice Pudding

My aunt-in-law is a noted cook and her *payesh* is something all our friends look forward to. This is her recipe.

5 litres milk
2 tins condensed milk
100 gms sugar
raisins as liked
100 gms almonds and pistachios, chopped
2–3 green cardamoms, powdered
2 bay leaves
100 gms rice

Place milk in a large pan or *dekchi*. Add the 2 tins condensed milk and bring to a boil. Continue until contents of pan are reduced by at least a third if not more.

Then wash and add the rice. Continue boiling, stirring from time to time, until the rice is just done.

Now add sugar, raisins, chopped almonds and pistachios, stir and cook for another 15–20 minutes.

Sprinkle powdered cardamom over *payesh* and remove from fire.

Pour into serving bowl and cool in refrigerator before serving.

Colour
Creamy
Texture
Grainy, thick
Flavour
Caramel, sweet

Darbesh

Sweetmeat Balls

Bondé made from 250 gms besan (chick-pea flour)
2 tablespoons khoa kheer/milk solids
2 tablespoons raisins, cleaned and soaked
a few pistachio nuts, soaked, peeled and minced fine
4 cups sugar*
4 cups water*

*combine and reduce to a thick syrup

Darbesh is made from *Bondé* (see page 195)

While *Bondé* is still warm, pour over it the thick syrup. Stir well. Add 2 tablespoons *khoa kheer* (near-dry thickened milk), 2 tablespoons raisins and the pistachios.

You may, if you wish, fry these three extra ingredients in a teaspoon of *ghee* before adding to the *Bondé*.

Now using your fingers, form *Bondé* into balls—the size of a table tennis ball or larger.

The balls of *Bondé* with the addition of *khoa kheer*, raisins and pistachio nuts are called 'Darbesh'.

A good accompaniment with: *Misti Doi*

Chhanar Payesh

Fresh Cottage Cheese Pudding

250 gms chhana. (fresh cottage
  cheese), crumbled coarsely
60 gms. sugar*
100 ml water*
1 litre milk
10 gms pistachio nuts, chopped
  fine
10 gms raisins—picked, washed
  and soaked to soften
2–3 drops rose water (optional)
a few rose petals (optional)

*combine and reduce to a thick
  syrup of hard ball consistency.

Place the *chhana* in a large bowl, and pour hot syrup into it a little at a time blending thoroughly after each addition. Continue until all the syrup is used. Cover the bowl and set aside.

In a large *dekchi*, boil the milk until reduced to half. Cool the milk till just warm.

Add the milk, a little at a time, to the *chhana* syrup mixture, stirring vigorously all the time, until all the milk is mixed in with the *chhana*.

Pour into a suitable sized serving bowl. Decorate with chopped pistachios, raisins and rose petals. Sprinkle with rose water.

Chill and serve.

The *Chhanar Payesh* may also be set in individual bowls.

Serves: 4–6

Rosogollar Payesh

1½ litres milk
20 rosogollas—without syrup
  (may be halved)
nuts and raisins for decoration.

Boil and reduce the milk to half, stirring all the time.

Cool thickened milk until warm. Add 20 *rossogol-las*. Decorate with nuts and raisins.

Chill and serve.

Serves: 4–6

Aam Kheer

Mango Custard

1½ litres milk
60 gms sugar
1 kg. good quality ripe mangoes,
    peeled and cut into 1 inch
    cubes.

Boil milk and sugar together until reduced to half.
Combine lukewarm thickened milk and mango. Chill.

Serves: 10–12

Sandesh

To make good *sandesh* is an art perfected after years of practice. There are a number of varieties of *sandesh* and it is made with various flavours such as *Aam Sandesh, Kamlanebur Sandesh, Notun Gurer Sandesh, Chocolate Sandesh*, etc. The texture of the *sandesh* can also vary. It can be a hard or *Kaurapak Sandesh* or the normal soft variety. The easiest way to mould a *sandesh* is to form into balls but specially carved wooden moulds are available for making *sandesh*.

500 gms chhana
375 gms sugar

Knead or grind the *chhana* into a fine paste.

In a *karai*, over a mild heat, fry together the *chhana* and sugar, stirring all the time. When the mixture leaves the sides of the pan and the sugar has melted, remove from fire.

While still warm, divide into equal portions and form into balls or press into moulds to shape.

Makes: 25 large sandesh

Rosogolla

1/2 kg chhana, with all the whey
    squeezed out
10 gms flour
10 gms sugar
4 drops essence of rose or rose
    water
35 1/4 inch pieces of palm candy
10 gms cardamom, peeled and
    seeds separated
1 kg sugar*
1 1/2 litres. water (6 cups)*
250 ml hot water

*boil and reduce to a thick syrup
    of hard ball consistency.

Knead the *chhana* into a pliable paste, adding the 4 drops essence of rose and flour.

When *chhana* leaves the sides of the dish, add sugar and knead lightly.

Divide *chhana* in 35 pieces.

Insert a piece of palm candy and a cardamom seed into the centre of each piece and roll in the palms to form balls.

Heat sugar syrup till it comes to the boil.

Add the *chhana* balls to the syrup ensuring that they do not touch each other.

Continue cooking for about 20 minutes adding some hot water from time to time to prevent the sugar syrup from becoming too thick. Remove from fire and cool. Transfer to bowl and serve with the syrup. Keeps for a couple of days in the refrigerator.

Note: Syrup must always be kept at a brisk boil while cooking. To test if *rosogolla* is cooked, drop a cooked *rosogolla* into a glass of water. It will sink to the bottom.

Makes: 35 pieces

Pressure Cooker Rosogolla

1/2 kg chhana, with all the whey
    squeezed out.
10 gms sugar
30 gms fine rice flour or
    arrowroot powder
35 1/4 inch pieces of palm candy
1/2 kg sugar
750 ml water
4 drops rosewater

Knead *chhana* and flour into a fine paste. Continue kneading till *chhana* stops sticking to the basin.

Lightly knead in sugar.

Divide into 35 equal portions and roll into smooth balls. Cover with a wet cloth and let stand for half an hour.

Boil and reduce sugar and water to a thick syrup in pressure cooker.

When it is boiling briskly, add the *chhana* balls, put lid and cook for 5 minutes.

DO NOT USE ANY WEIGHT.

Sprinkle with rosewater.

Note: It may be necessary to cook the *rosogollas* in 2 lots as they should be spaced at least 1 inch apart.

Lady Kenny

Lady Canning

Indeed an unusual name for a Bengali sweetmeat dish. It can boast of a historical background. When Calcutta was the capital and Lord Canning was Viceroy of India, his wife, Lady Canning, undertook a visit to a *mofussil* town in Bengal. Great preparations were made to receive Her Excellency and special sweetmeats prepared. This particular dish was appreciated by the Lady and was renamed in her honour, but has finally come to be known locally as 'Lady Kenny'.

The *Pantua* and *Lady Kenny* are very similar, except that the latter is much larger and coated in castor sugar.

750 gms chhana or panir
150 gms suji or semolina
1 teaspoon pure ghee
½ kg ghee for frying
thick sugar syrup made from boiling ½ kg
sugar with 1 cup water
100 gms castor sugar
20 raisins, washed and soaked in water, then dried

Knead the *chhana, suji* and a teaspoon of pure *ghee* to make a smooth dough. Sprinkle the large grain sugar and knead lightly.

Divide the *chhana* into approximately 20 portions. Roll to form balls.

Stuff each ball with a raisin and roll in the palms of the hands until quite round.

In a *karai* heat the *ghee* and when hot (400°F), fry the balls of *chhana* 2 or 3 at a time until quite brown. Keep temperature constant.

Remove with a slotted spoon.

Drain on paper.

Immerse in prepared syrup leaving for an hour and a half.

Sprinkle castor sugar on a piece of waxed paper or plate.

Remove *Lady Kennys* from syrup one at a time and roll in sugar to coat and place in serving bowl or dish.

Serve at room temperature.

Makes: 20

Pantua

750 gms chhana or panir
150 gms suji or semolina
1 teaspoon pure ghee
½ kg ghee for frying
thick sugar syrup made from boil-
　　ing ½ kg sugar with 1 cup
　　water
20 raisins, washed and soaked in
　　water, then dried
2 black cardamoms, peeled and
　　seeds crushed
1 litre milk, reduced to milk
　　solids (khoa kheer)
1 kg sugar*
1 kg water*
1 tablespoon large grain sugar for
　　chhana

*reduced to a thin syrup

Knead the chhana, suji and a teaspoon of pure ghee to make a smooth dough. Sprinkle large grain sugar and knead lightly.

Divide the chhana into approximately 20 portions. Roll to form balls.

Combine milk solids and crushed cardamom, make into 20 tiny balls. Stuff each chhana ball with a kheer centre, and a raisin.

In a karai heat the ghee and when hot (400°F), fry the balls of chhana 2 or 3 at a time until quite brown. Keep temperature constant.

Remove with a slotted spoon.

Drain on paper.

Immerse in prepared thin syrup leaving for an hour and a half. Remove and then serve in thick syrup.

Makes: 20

Chhanar Jilipi

750 gms chhana or panir
150 gms suji or semolina
1 teaspoon pure ghee
½ kg ghee for frying
thick sugar syrup made from boil-
　　ing ½ kg sugar with 1 cup
　　water
2 black cardamoms, peeled and
　　seeds crushed
1 litre milk, reduced to milk
　　solids (khoa kheer)
1 kg. sugar*
1 ltr. water*

*reduced to thin syrup

Knead the chhana, suji and a teaspoon of pure ghee to make a smooth dough

Fill chhana in pastry bag using a choux pastry nozzle, pipe out whirls on the back of a slotted spoon.

In a karai heat the ghee and when hot (400°F), fry the whirls of chhana 2 or 3 at a time until quite brown. Keep temperature constant.

Remove with a slotted spoon.

Drain on paper.

Immerse in prepared thin syrup leaving for an hour and a half. Remove and then serve in thick syrup.

Makes: 20

Chitrokoot

500 gms chhana or panir
150 gms suji or semolina
250 gms khoa kheer (milk solids)
1 teaspoon pure ghee
½ kg ghee for frying
thick sugar syrup made from boil-
    ing ½ kg sugar with 1 cup
    water
100 gms castor sugar
⅛ teaspoon powdered mace.
1 tablespoon large grain sugar for
    chhana

Follow instructions for making *Lady Kenny* except knead into dough *khoa kheer* and mace. Shape into squares by putting dough into a half inch thick rectangle and cutting into 1½–2 inch squares or diamonds.

Colour
Dark brown, brown
Shape: Lady Kenny—round
Pantua—round
Chitrokoot—Square or diamond
Chhanar Jilipi—round whirls.
Texture / Consistency
Smooth and spongy with a thick centre.
Flavour
Creamy, caramel, sweet.

Malpoa

Yogurt Fritters in Syrup

240 gms. flour
180 ml. dahi
water as required
•3–4 large black cardamoms–peel
    and separate seeds
ghee for frying malpoas
250 gms. sugar*
500 ml. water*

*Boiled together to form a
    medium thick syrup

Whisk together the flour and *dahi* adding enough water to make a thick batter. Stir in the cardamom seeds. Let stand for 1 hour.

Heat *ghee* in a small *karai* or a frypan for deep frying.

Drop one tablespoon batter at a time into mildly simmering *ghee*.

The batter spreads to make *malpoas* of five inch diameter.

Fry till brown and crisp at the edges.

Remove from *ghee* with slotted spoon, draining off as much *ghee* as possible.

Soak in prepared syrup.

Serve in syrup.

Note: I recommend the use of a non-stick *karai* or frypan.

Kheerer Malpoa

Condensed Milk Fritters in Syrup

½ litre thickened milk (kheer)
50 gms semolina
200 ml milk (approx 1 cup)
ghee for deep frying malpoas
240 gms sugar*
500 ml water*

*boiled together to form a
    medium thick syrup

Mix the semolina and half a cup of milk.
    Blend in the thickened milk.
    Add enough milk to make a thick batter.
    Heat *ghee* in a *karai* and fry *Kheer Malpoas* as described in 'Malpoa'.

Variation:
half litre *khoa kheer* may be used instead of ordinary *kheer*, in which case the quantity of milk should be adjusted.

Colour
Cream with brown edges.
Texture / Consistency.
Soft centred, crisp at the edge, syrupy.
Flavour
Sweet with a slight sour taste.

Make: 10 Malpoas

Patishapta

Pancakes with Coconut filling

For Patishapta:
120 gms flour
60 gms rice flour or finely
powdered rice
1/8 teaspoon sodium bicarbonate
250 ml milk
ghee for shallow frying.

For Filling:
100 gms fresh coconut, grated
(approx. 100 gms coconut meat)
100 gms sugar
100 gms thickened milk/kheer or
1/2 cup condensed milk (omit
sugar if used)
Nuts and raisins, chopped and
added to filling (optional)

In a bowl mix flour, rice flour and bicarbonate of soda with milk. Mix to a smooth batter and set aside for half an hour.

In a *karai*, stir together the coconut, sugar and milk until they adhere together in a soft moist mass. Remove *karai* from the fire and allow filling to cool.

Heat a 6-inch frying pan and grease with a drop of *ghee*. Swirl pan around so that it is evenly coated with the hot *ghee*.

Drop 2 tablespoons batter into the frying pan and swirl pan around to coat evenly with batter.

Allow batter to set and cook until underside of *Patishapta* or Pancake is turning brown.

With teaspoon spread filling half-inch wide across *Patishapta* at one end.

Fold *Patishapta* over filling and roll over to the other end. Remove from pan.

Serve hot or cold.

Note: I recommend using a non-stick pan

Colour
Creamy brown
Texture/Consistency
Thin, with grainy filling.
Flavour
Coconuts & pancake.

Makes: 12–16 Patishaptas

Misti Alurpuli

Sweet Potato Balls with Coconut filling in Syrup

1 kg sweet potatoes, boiled***
  peeled and mashed
50 gms flour***
200 gms fresh coconut, grated*
100 gms thickened milk*
100 gms sugar*
50 gms raisins, picked, washed
  and soaked in water*
ghee for frying*
350 gms. sugar**
750 ml water**

*For filling
**For syrup
***For dough

To make Syrup:
Heat sugar and water in a pan. Bring to boil and thicken to soft ball consistency.

To make Filling:
In a *karai* fry together the ingredients for filling until sugar and *kheer* are completely blended with coconut and all the moisture from the coconut has evaporated and it is lightly browned.

To make Dough:
Add enough flour to the sweet potatoes so that it is firm enough to hold.

To make Puli:
Divide sweet potatoes into 12 equal portions. Then form into rounds. Flour hands as you work.

Form a cup in the palm of your hand with the round sweet potatoes and stuff with coconut *kheer* filling. Close cup. Remould into rounds and then mould into a torpedo shape with your fingers.

Heat *ghee* in a *karai*.

Deep fry in simmering *ghee* until lightly browned.

Drain off as much *ghee* as possible on paper but while still hot, place in syrup and leave for several hours before serving.

Colour
Dark brown
Texture / Consistency
Smooth casing with grainy filling.
Soft and dripping with syrup.
Flavour
Sweet potato and coconut cream flavour.
Sweet.

Makes: 12 Pulis

Gokul Pitha

Coconut Cakes in Syrup

200 gms coconut, grated.*
2 litres milk, boiled and reduced
   to 2 cup kheer*
50 gms sugar to add to coconut
   milk cakes*
150 gms flour**
200 ml water**
40 gms ghee**
1/8 teaspoon sodium bicarbonate**
250 gms sugar***
500 ml water***
ghee for deep frying.

*for filling
**blend to make a thick batter
***for syrup

To make Syrup
Heat the sugar and water in a *dekchi*. Simmer until syrup is of a medium thick consistency. Remove from fire and cool. Syrup should be of soft ball consistency.

To make Filling:
In a *karai*, fry the coconut, *kheer* and sugar together until well-blended to make filling. Continue frying stirring all the time so that it does not catch at the bottom of the pan, cook, stirring until coconut, *kheer* and sugar come together in a mass. Remove from fire.

To make Gokul Pitha:
Divide *coconut-kheer* mixture into 25 portions.
   First roll into balls and then flatten between the palms of hands to form cakes. You may have to powder your hands with flour for ease in forming the cakes.
   Heat *ghee* in a *karai* for deep frying.
   Coat a few coconut-milk cakes at a time in the prepared batter.
   Deep fry until a rich golden brown.
   Remove from pan with slotted spoon.
   Drain on paper for a couple of minutes and while still quite hot, immerse in the syrup.

Colour
Golden, brown
Texture / Consistency
Solid, crisp and soft
Flavour
Rich coconut cream taste, sweet.

Makes: 25 Pithas

Narkeler Naru

Coconut Cakes

200 gms fresh coconut, grated
1 litre milk, boiled and reduced
    to ¾ cup kheer
180 gms sugar

Mix the coconut, sugar and *kheer* together in a *karai*
Set *karai* on a medium fire.

Stir-fry until the coconut, sugar and *kheer* are well
blended and dry enough to adhere together. Remove
from fire while still slightly moist.

Divide into 12 portions and form into balls. Leave
to set and serve cold.

Variation I:
After making *Narkeler Naru*, stuff with a little *khoa
kheer* and finely chopped pistachios. Remould into
balls and leave to set.

Variation II:
Substitute condensed milk for fresh milk. Omit sugar.

Colour
Cream
Texture / Consistency
Granular and set semi-hard
Flavour
Coconut cream.

Makes: 12 Narus

PAAN

BETEL LEAF

Pan and Moshla

Pan is the leaf of a creeping plant now known as Betel vine and traditionally eaten after a meal as a digestive. Because it is usually eaten with the addition of *supari* or betel nut, it is commonly called Betel leaf. Various spices are added according to taste. Standard preparation includes:

Supari (betel nut)

Khoyer (catechu)

Chun (quick lime)

Khoyer and *chun* are usually in the form of a paste which is smeared on the leaf, while other ingredients are added dry in small quantitites—usually just a pinch of each. Other spices commonly added are:

Elachi (cardamom—seeds of the large black variety are preferred for *pan* and *moshla*)

Mouri (aniseed)

Menthol (peppermint)

Narkol (coconut)

Misti supari (sweetened betel nut)

Pan can become an addiction when a quantity of *tamak* (tobacco) is used in the formula in the form of *jarda* or *dokta*.

Jarda: Powdered tobacco leaf, obtainable in different strengths.

Dokta: Tobacco leaf, aniseed, coriander, *garam masala*—all powdered together.

Chewing *pan* gives the typical redness to lips and tongue and taken in excess, badly stains the teeth.

Moshla

Many people like to have *moshla* (spices) without pan. There are of course many variations and/or additions according to taste. The following formula is a fairly standard one:

2 parts *Dhoner chal* (split coriander seed)

1 part *Mouri*

½ part *Elachi*

½ part *Juan*

All ingredients are pan roasted separately and mixed together. It can be kept reasonably fresh and crispy stored in an airtight container. It can also be successfully revived if damp, by re-roasting on a dry *tawa* or frying pan.

Optional additions: Finely cut *supari* or small pieces of *misri* (crystalline sugar).

Index

Achar, Ambal, Chutney & Tauk, 175-88
Chutneys & Pickles

Aam Jhol, 177
Aam Kasondi, 177
Aamer Chutney (1), 178
Aamer Chutney (2), 179
Aamer Misti Achar, 179
Mango Murabba, 188
Alubokhara Chutney, 180
Anaras Chutney, 180
Choto Chingri Sambal, 181
Lankar Achar, 182
Lau Ba Peper Chutney, 183
Maacher Dimer Tauk, 184
Tetul Gola, 185
Tomato Chutney, 186
Tomato Kasondi, 187
Topa Kooler Ambal, 188

Anglo-Indian Recipes 161-74
Anglo-Indian Dishes of Bengal

Alu Chop, 162
Coorkit, 163
Crumb Chops, 164
Fish Moulee, 165
Hilsa Fish Fry, 165
Jhal Ferazi, 166
Mince Curry, 167
Murgi Cutlet, 168
Mutton Cutlet, 169
Mutton Cutlet Curry, 169
Pantaras, 170
Poached Eggs in tomato gravy, 171
Pork Vindaloo, 172

Smoked Hilsa, 173
Tomato Farci, 174

Aunno, 14-22
Cereals

Boiled Rice, 15
Bahu Khuda, 17
Ghee Bhaat, 18
Khichuri, 19
Luchi, 20
Porota, 21
Radhaballobhi Luchi, 22

Dal, 24-34
Pulses and legumes

Aurhor Dal with Vegetables, 25
Cholar Dal, 26
Dal Chenchki, 27
Dhokar Dalna, 28
Ghugni, 29
Kalai Dal, 30
Matarsutir Dal, 31
Misti Sona Moog Dal, 32
Muro Dal, 33
Musur Dal, 34
Tauk Dal, 34

Jalkhabar, 189-96
Snacks

Alu Kabli, 190
Chire Bhaja, 191
Chirer Pulao, 191
Elo-Jhelo, 192

Jibe-Goja, 193
Matarsutir Kochuri, 194
Mohan Bhog, 194
Murir Moa, 195
Nimki, 195
Shingara, 196
Tel-Muri, 196

Maach, 98-140
Fish

Asto Bekti Maacher Dom, 108
Baked Butter Bekti with Saffron Rice, 109
Chingri-Alu-Phulkopir Dalna, 124
Chingri Bharta, 119
Chingri Bhate, 128
Chingri Cutlet, 120
Chingri Cutlet Curry, 121, 122
Chingri Daab, 129
Chingri Dhokar Dom, 126
Chingri Maacher Kabiraji Cutlet, 123
Chingri Maacher Paturi, 127
Chingri Malai, 133
Chingri Vindaloo, 135
Chitol Maacher Mondo, 112
Choto Chingrir Chorchori, 125
Choto Chingri Kofta, 130
Choto Chingri Kofta Curry, 131-32
Doi Maach, 118
Elish Maach, 113
Elish Bhaja, 114
Elish Maacher Kancha Jhol, 115
Elish Maacher Paturi, 117
Elish Maacher Tauk Jhol, 116
Elish Sorse Jhol, 115
Elish Tetul, 114
Galda Chingri Bhaja, 136
Galda Chingrir Curry, 137
Galda Chingri Bhaja, 136
Galda Chingrir Curry, 137
Ganga-Jamuna, 106
Kakkrar Chorchori, 138
Kakkrar Curry, 139
Kethor Jhol, 140
Koi Maacher Chorchori, 111

Maacher Jhol, 99
Maacher Sorse Jhol, 101
Muri Ghanto, 107
Narkel Chingri Bharta, 119
Parshe Maacher Jhal, 110
Pixie's Special, 105
Rabeya's Prawn & Bamboo Shoot Curry, 134
Rui Maacher Curry, 101
Rui Maacher Jhol, 100
Rui Maacher Kalia, 103
Rui Maacher Korma, 102
Rui Maacher Doi Maach, 104

Misti, 197-212
Sweets

Aam Kheer, 203
Bhapa Doi, 199
Bonde, 199
Chhanar Jilipi, 206
Chhanar Payesh, 202
Chitrokoot, 207
Darbesh, 201
Gokul Pitha, 211
Jethima's Payesh for a crowd, 201
Kheerer Malpoa, 208
Lady Kenny, 205
Malpoa, 207
Misti Alurpuli, 210
Narkeler Naru, 212
Pantua, 206
Patishpta, 209
Payesh, 200
Pressure Cooker Rosogolla, 204
Rosogolla, 204
Rosogollar Payesh, 202
Sandesh, 203

Mangsho, Murgi O Dim, 142-60
Chicken, Eggs & Meat

Dimer Bharta, 159
Dimer Bora, 159
Dimer Curry, 160
Husseini Curry, 150

Kabab, 151
Mangsho-Capsicum-Piaj Curry, 155
Mangsho Dopiaza, 149
Mangsho-O-Lal Kumro, 154
Mangshor Curry, 144, 145, 146
Mangshor Ghugni, 152, 153
Mangshor Gota Mashla, 148
Mangshor Kofta Curry, 147
Murgi Curry, 155
Murgi Gota Moshla, 157
Murgi Korma, 156
Murgi Malal, 156
Murgi and Bansher Korol, 158
Omelette Curry, 160
Pathar Jhol, 143

Paan and Moshla, 214

Tarkari, 35-96
Vegetables

Alu Potoler Dalna, 67
Alu Phulkopir Dalna, 68
Alu Piajer Chorchori, 53
Alur Dom, 65, 66
Bandhakopir Dalna, 69
Bandhakopir Misti Dalna, 63
Bati Chorchori, 54
Begun Sorse, 59

BHAJA

Alu Bhaja, 38
Begun Bhaja, 38
Beshon Bhaja, 39
Bangla Pan, 35
Brinjal, 42, 58, 59
Capsicum, 35
Cauliflower, 50, 61
Cucumber, 35
Green Chillies, 35
Khosha Bhaja, 38
Ladies' Finger, 35, 59
Phuluri, 40
Potatoes, 38, 41, 43, 47, 53, 65-68

Red Pumpkin, 44, 45, 60, 78
Spinach, 52, 80
Sweet Potatoes, 35

BHATE OR PORA

Alu Bhate, 41
Begun Pora, 42
Kumro or Red Pumpkin Bhate, 41
Banana Plant – Thor, Mocha O Kanchkola, 81

BORA

Alu Bora, 43
Narkel Bora, 43
Postor Bora, 44
Chhanar Dalna, 70
Chhanar Dolma, 96
Chhanar Kalia, 74

CHORCHORI & CHANCHRA

Chingri Dolma, 90
Dharosh or Bhindi Chorchori, 55
Dharosh or Bhindi Sorse, 59
Doi Begun, 88
Doi Potol, 89

DOLMAS

Alu Posto, 47
Dolma Curry, 92
Enchorer Dalna, 71
Enchorer Kalia, 75
Fish Dolma, 91
Jhinge Chingri, 76, 77
Jhinge Kumro Paturi, 60
Jhinge Posto, 47
Kanchkolar Cutlet, 87
Kanchkolar Cutlet Curry, 88
Khosha Chorchori, 55
Kochu Sager Ghanto, 48
Kopir Muri Ghanto, 50
Kumro Bothi, 72
Kumro Chenchki, 44

Kumror Chhokka, 45
Kumro Chingri, 78
Lau Chingri, 79
Lauer Misti Dalna, 63
Lau Ghanto, 49
Misti Dalna, 64
Mangshor Dolma, 93, 94, 95
Mocha, 84
Mochar Ghanto, 85
Mochar Paturi, 86
Monama, 61
Moricher Jhol, 46
Mulor Ghanto, 51

Palong Chingri, 80
Palong Sager Ghanto, 52
Potoler Dolma, 90
Peper Dalna, 73
Pui Sager Chorchori, 56
Sajne Dantar Chorchori, 57
Sajne Sorse, 62
Sheem Begun Chorchori, 58
Sheem Sorse, 62
Shukto, 37
Thor, 81
Thor Chenchki, 82
Thorer Ghanto, 83